THE PERSON IN THE MIRROR

Also by George A. Goens

Civility Lost: The Media, Politics, and Education

It's Not My Fault: Victim Mentality and Becoming Response-able

The Fog of Reform: Getting Back to a Place Called School

Straitjacket: How Overregulation Stifles Creativity and Innovation in Education

Resilient Leadership for Turbulent Times: A Guide to Thriving in the Face of Adversity

Soft Leadership for Hard Times

THE PERSON IN THE MIRROR

Education and the Search for Self and Meaning

George A. Goens

ROWMAN & LITTLEFIELD
Lanham • Boulder • New York • London

Published by Rowman & Littlefield
An imprint of The Rowman & Littlefield Publishing Group, Inc.
4501 Forbes Boulevard, Suite 200, Lanham, Maryland 20706
www.rowman.com

6 Tinworth Street, London SE11 5AL, United Kingdom

British Library Cataloguing in Publication Information Available

Library of Congress Control Number: 2019949265

Library of Congress Cataloguing-in-Publication Data Is Available
ISBN 978-1-4758-4716-1 (cloth: alk. paper)
ISBN 978-1-4758-4717-8 (electronic)

♾ ™ The paper used in this publication meets the minimum requirements of American National Standard for Information Sciences Permanence of Paper for Printed Library Materials, ANSI/NISO Z39.48-1992.

For . . .

. . . my father, Earl Goens, who died when I was four years old. I miss him to this day.

. . . my uncles Zig, Bill, and Ed, for the care, experiences, and advice they shared with me in my childhood.

. . . my mother, Stephanie Goens, who raised two children and taught me and my sister about responsibility, hard work, and resilience.

. . . Marilyn, for helping me to continue to answer the question "Who am I?"

CONTENTS

PREFACE

"**P**omp and Circumstance" welcomed the five hundred graduates, all decked out in black ceremonial caps and gowns, as they made their way down the aisle to their seats, which were aligned in rows in the center of the basketball arena. Parents scanned the line and some let out a yelp as they identified their loved one. Once seated, the graduates were difficult to recognize as individuals. It was a class: same caps, same gowns, same diplomas.

A big day was at hand for all of the students as they sat together for the last time before they would move ahead with their individual lives, scattering for education, jobs, military service, travel, or other endeavors. Today was the last day they were all together as a class.

The student who had the second-highest grade point average (GPA) gave a speech and stated, "We are not a number," as she cited the test metrics and GPAs that are used in schools to characterize students. Her speech was civil, clear, respectfully delivered, but poignant. We are individuals, not metrics, she asserted; numbers do not describe us.

The closing speaker, the school board president, took an expected path, providing statistics on the ranking of the school in the state, the collective GPAs, the percentage of students graduating, the ranking and achievements of sports teams and other school clubs and activities. All data about the success, performance, and excellence of the school confirmed that the class was accomplished and ready for the next step in life.

The student and board member presented contrasting perspectives. While students sat in a mass of uniformity, in reality, each one was unique and unlike the other 499 students sitting nearby. All were part of a class, but each was an individual with distinctive dreams, talents, aspirations, and futures. Group statistics did not and do not describe any individual student in any specific or meaningful way. Uniqueness is immune to metrical description.

All people—those graduates, their teachers and administrators, and everyone in the stadium—are bound together by their uniqueness. No one is special or above the others, but each is one-of-a-kind, distinctive, and never to be duplicated. Creativity, independence, and individuality are the keystones by which each life flows and follows a course unlike that of others.

However, that day each graduate confronted the same singular question that all must answer: "Who am I?" No right or wrong answer exists for that question, which can be said to truly encompass a person's individuality. In fact, it was probably never directly raised in class, yet it is the most significant one affecting the entirety of the students' lives. How did their elementary and secondary education prepare them, if at all, to answer it?

In addition, the graduates must soon confront another significant question as they begin the next phase of their life: "Why am I here?" For some, the answer seems clear at this point, for others there is a vague idea, and for many it is uncertain and unclear. However, the question will be raised, perhaps a number of times.

Actually, these two questions will be constants in the students' lives, in each phase and in every decade, including old age. The answers may differ as the individuals continue to learn about themselves through their successes, failures, and individual choices. In addition, life and its unexpected turns of fate will affect their outlook and development. Experiences will shape them and hopefully help them find greater self-understanding and direction. The answers to those two questions are as different as the individuals themselves.

Simple answers to "Who am I?" and "Why am I here?" do not exist. How people perceive and determine the context and choices they face will shape their answers. Education and school can provide a safe space and intellectual and emotional frameworks in which to consider and contemplate them, but each individual is responsible to find the answer to those basic questions of life.

How do individuals gain the wisdom to answer the solitary question—Who am I?—that they alone must answer. Only when they have done so can they answer the second question, Why am I here? Criteria for assessing these queries go far beyond quantitative tests and measurements. No tests, technology, or artificial intelligence will help them. Ultimately, only the individual can determine whether he or she is on the right course to live a fulfilling life.

What do students need to begin the journey to contemplate and answer those questions? The journey, an individual and personal one continuing throughout life, relies on understanding great ideas, values, and ethics, as well as on exploring and understanding personal strengths, fears, and attitudes. Self-understanding and self-identity require reflection and a bit of courage. Coming to terms with oneself takes time and is not always easy.

A corollary question is, How does society unleash the potential of the human mind and spirit? What does it take? Many would say education is the answer, but what kind of education? Is it the well from which all knowledge and wisdom is derived? What personal impact can each individual have on society and the greater good?

Education reform proposals focus on certain purposes: employment, social and civic duties, economic success, skill development, communication, and relationships. Technology is celebrated. Achievement on standardized tests and other measurements are a priority. Much in the way of education reform is focused on metrics, none of which can measure the self or character.

Eventually children must grow to understand that they are in full control of how they respond to all situations, positive or negative. Life doesn't just happen to them. Sure, fate is in play at times, but each individual has the choice on how to react to what evolves. People actually create their life by the choices and responses they make as individuals.

Living a life is a "one time only" experience. There are no second chances. Some individuals think their lives are preset, that fate establishes the events and the pathway. While fate presents some circumstances, individuals interpret and respond to them in different ways. Unexpected events open or close doors and opportunities, and some understand that their decisions and reactions establish their life's course and outcomes.

As Eleanor Roosevelt stated, "The purpose of life, after all, is to live it, to taste experiences to the utmost, to reach out eagerly and without fear for newer and richer experiences."

This is not a how-to book. There is no simple recipe for understanding oneself. Each person must take the journey and follow his or her individual path. The book, however, does provide perspective and addresses the concepts that are at play and that everyone confronts in this lifetime journey to finding purpose and meaning.

Unless otherwise indicated, the poems at the end of each chapter are my own. The poems were written over a considerable period of time and reflect the issues that one faces in life that open doors to insight and perspective.

I

THE MIRROR

If you live each day as if it was your last, someday you'll most certainly be right.

—Steve Jobs

We are so afraid of silence that we chase ourselves from one event to the next in order not to spend a moment alone with ourselves, in order not to have to look at ourselves in the mirror.

—Dietrich Bonhoeffer

Who are you? People generally respond by giving their name, line of work, and where they live—name, rank, and serial number—all generic information without much depth or insight, really. In private moments, however, the answer to that question may be more complicated.

Looking inside is not always easy, and the mirror does not reveal a person's essence. External appearance or behavior does not get to the heart of the matter. There is a person within whom others cannot see beyond the external impression. Personality and passion are not physically visible. What you see may not be what you get.

In the morning, looking closely into the mirror and examining facial contours and features, what would be the response to the question, Who are you? Seeing the image may spur a more introspective response, reflecting unexpressed feelings, ambitions, fears, uncertainty, and insecurity. Self-doubts may reside next to ambitions. Sadness may be masked by an extroverted exterior personality that can only be seen in the depth of one's eyes.

Society emphasizes physical appearance and assumes that it communicates character and personality. The issue is, how do others view and interpret that image in the mirror? How would friends and family perceive that person? Parents and relatives? Social or peer groups? Employers and colleagues? The physical image may not correlate at all with who the person really is as a human being. A beautiful physique may carry an inconsiderate, dishonest, and insincere personality. Physical attractiveness does not translate into a caring and good person.

The stereotypes of older people or of racial or ethnic groups may be distant from the individual selves that live within the outer shell. Are there important things about a person that can be discerned through appearance and expressions? How often do we draw conclusions based on photographs or images? A picture may be "worth a thousand words," but none of them may be accurate or reliable. The mind, spirit, heart, and soul cannot be photographed; they are only visible in the person's "being"—or essential nature.

People are much more than their bodies, which mature with time and eventually age, and they may be far different people mentally and philosophically than what their bodies might suggest. The youthful face slowly evolves into a wrinkled one, and the firm physique eventually creaks with stiffened joints and flaccid muscles. The person inside, however, may be fundamentally different in character, personality, or moral disposition than the external shell. Other people's views may be contrary to a person's self-image. They may be poles apart—even at odds.

Many children are tightly focused on their physiques and personal appearance. Sometimes, particularly in early adolescence, both boys and girls are self-conscious about height, weight, and appearance. Media imagery of perfect bodies, based on contemporary views of manhood and womanhood, can become obsessive and invalid.

Bodies mature and age at different rates. An eighth-grade graduation picture illustrates the diversity of children's physical stature. Some boys are six feet tall and ambling, and others are much shorter and look like they are sixth graders. Puberty is not a switch that flips on at a specific time. The same is true for girls as they develop. Eventually, growth takes place, and everyone reaches physical maturity.

Aging is one continuing change in life that everyone confronts, even though plastic surgery and the fashion industry may think otherwise.

Maintaining youth is a lost cause: aging is inescapable, unavoidable, and can be an exhilarating and fulfilling part of life.

Our society also categorizes people. Some are so-called stars and icons; there is even a bizarre concept of royalty in this day and age. Others are common people: neighbors, friends, colleagues, and relatives. Some identify themselves by ethnic, fiscal, racial, or sexual classification. For others, their profession brings a perspective and identity based on their responsibilities and the image it represents. Those identities, however, may not be complex enough to accurately describe the individual beyond their limits.

Multiple selves may live within the same physical body. Individuals can appear to be very different people at work than at home or socially. Their external personality may not be in harmony with their inner being. A confident outer image may camouflage inner insecurities. Individuals may role-play—be inauthentic—and change their personality and even their character in response to circumstances, social expectations, or people.

THE IMMEASURABLES

What cannot be observed is the person's mind and heart. The mirror is blank when it comes to looking inside a person. The mind cannot be physically observed, only represented in decisions and actions. Thoughts, ideas, assessments, and analysis become evident in people's cognitive behavior. Cognitive ability and learning are essential in life and can be tested or observed. The inner soul and spirit of a person, however, cannot be captured in any physical form or measured metrically.

Confronting oneself is a continual progression. At one time or another, everyone has to answer, "Who am I?" Actually, it is a consistent question throughout all stages of life. Events and decisions can create uncertainty and doubt. Self-image may conflict with reality. Who the person is may change over time due to experiences and learning and self-understanding. Age and exploits bring different perspectives and insight.

How many selves are there within a person? Are they authentic to one's self-identity and principles and values? The answer relies on whether the person knows the self within. Finding and understanding who one is results in authenticity—the congruence between self, behavior, and personality. What others want is irrelevant to fulfilling one's ambitions and passions.

The second important question is, "Why am I here?" Does occupation, address, or other demographic information describe why people are here? Is a job the reason? What drives life? Is there a self-defined destiny, or is there a preplanned future that is to be played out? What values and beliefs direct choices and decisions—and which ones are nonnegotiable?

The essence of these questions rests on the common desire to live a good and meaningful life. Meaning is not necessarily the same for all individuals. What does that suggest? Assessing one's or another's life is difficult, and there isn't one universal definition, formula, or algorithm for it. Do all people find meaning the same way, or does it depend on each individual?

Meaning is an intangible and cannot be easily measured. While schools and contemporary society worship on the altar of quantitative analysis, some of the most important questions in life are beyond metrics. What metric defines a person? A personality? A commitment? A sense of compassion? A life? What is the metric for determining whether a person has led a good life? Is there a statistic for compassion? Meaning? Creativity? Integrity? Self-understanding?

Quantitative measurements do not really exist for an individual. Test scores, IQs, bank accounts, or trophies do not signify the quality or significance of a life. These metrics do not always lead to a noble and fulfilling life, nor do they translate automatically into happiness, achievement, and purpose. Important aspects of life move beyond strictly cognitive intelligence or physical prowess. Life, throughout all its phases, calls upon other aspects—heart, emotions, creativity, desires, ideas, and purpose.

The mirror only shows an outward reflection—external and tangible—but does not provide a complete picture of individuals: their inner feelings and spirit within them, the humanness that arises in love and passion or in defense of principles and ethics. Moral character does not reveal itself in physical reflections but lives in a person's heart and soul, guides decisions, and arouses emotions.

Matters of heart, feelings, and emotions are powerful forces, often able to override reason and cognitive analyses and evaluation. Issues of love, fear, anger, sadness, and happiness are influential and affect an individual's physical and cognitive actions—it can be mind over matter. Emotion can eclipse reason. Matters of the heart are not dependent on physique or physical strength. The human spirit provides determination and moral strength far beyond physical stature and force. Heart often provides the foundation for commitment and dedication to overcome difficulties.

Mind and heart, however, are connected. As child psychiatrist Kyle Pruett stated, "Emotion and feeling . . . are what really drive learning most efficiently. Children who are in a good mood learn better."[1] This applies to people of all ages whose emotions direct their thinking and problem-solving abilities. At all stages, emotional tenor and internal feelings influence people's reactions to life experiences positively or negatively.

Ralph Waldo Emerson stated, "A man should learn to detach and watch that gleam of light which flashes across his mind from within, more than the luster of the firmament of bards and sages. Yet he dismisses without notice his thought, because it is his."[2] The gleam of light can be from one's "sixth sense," or intuition. Intuition is one of those things individuals refer to generally about decisions they made or did not make: "My intuition told me to . . . " or "I just had a feeling . . . ," and then they discuss how things worked to or not to their advantage, depending on whether or not they followed that internal voice.

The inner voice raises feelings not expressed openly and arising from instinct and impressions without hard or concrete information. Some consider it a source of wisdom and conscience. Inner voices may well provide contrary information as individuals contemplate circumstances. Intuition sometimes warns, critiques, and advises. But there are other forces at work as well.

Self-image develops not only from within but is also formed through social and peer pressure, family, and an array of other influences affecting ambitions, social contact, and conflict. Security can be bolstered or weakened through these interactions, and trust can be enhanced or destroyed. Fear can torpedo the spirit of adventure, and confidence can be weakened through failure.

Fear is a potent force, but not always a rational one. The poet David Whyte commented, "Fears are almost always irrational. You cannot reason them out of existence. If you could, they would have gone long ago."[3] Overcoming fear, however, can be a constructive and cogent influence that provides continued initiative, drive, and confidence.

Expectations of parents, peers, or others work in two ways: they either support an individual's passions and dreams or negate them. External expectations and standards can be vilifying unless the individual has a strong sense of self and understanding of who he or she is. Success depends on social competence, problem-solving skills, and emotional security, not on the expectations and prejudices of others.

Steve Jobs's quote puts all of this in perspective. He advised, "Your time is limited, so don't waste it living someone else's life. Don't be trapped by dogma—which is living with the results of other people's thinking. Don't let the noise of others' opinions drown out your own inner voice. And, most important, have the courage to follow your heart and intuition. They somehow already know what you truly want to become. Everything else is secondary."[4]

CARPE DIEM

Jobs's quote can be simplified to carpe diem—"seize the day"—because there is no time to waste: no day to squander. As individuals age, that reality cuts deeper into their core. In the movie *Dead Poets Society*, Robin Williams, as Mr. Keating, the instructor at Welton Academy, a prep school, stated, "Seize the day, boys, make your lives extraordinary." He later reasoned, "Because we are food for worms, lads. Because, believe it or not, each and every one of us in this room is, one day, gonna stop breathing, turn cold, and die."[5]

He was right on two scores: first, to actively pursue life, and second, to become uniquely who you are. There is no time to waste, and decisions matter. At times young people have a skewed view of how much time they have on earth and what they can do with it. They sometimes believe the time to act will come later, but sometimes it doesn't. The time may be now.

Some do not believe or understand they can live a life that is exceptional—filled with promise and achievement. In fact, that desire arises in every person and echoes throughout life. What some do not comprehend is that extraordinary lives are not simply about fame, notoriety, or titles, nor are they about money and possessions. Exceptional lives come cloaked in the intangibles of integrity, honor, and principles.

Finding oneself comes with gains and losses and successes and failures, individually as well as socially and collectively. Reality can be soft or harsh. Any worthwhile journey is going to have challenges: the road is not always straight, curves abound, and dead ends happen. An occasional fender bender might happen that forestalls rapid or immediate progress. Fortitude, however, coupled with desire can lead to self-fulfillment and purpose, even though goals and ambitions change with experience, insight, and understanding.

LIFE TRAJECTORIES

Sipping their coffee, Eddie and Julia talked about the future. Eddie said, "A while ago, I listened to a twenty-four-year-old describing his life's path: career promotions in yearly increments, a condo with a view, a new Beamer convertible by the time he's twenty-eight, and, of course, exciting dates. He seemed smart—"

Julia interrupted, "But certainly not wise."

"Yeah, I wonder how it worked out for him," Eddie laughed.

The twenty-four-year-old's youthful outlook doesn't really stack up. Subtle and muted nuances have significant and unexpected impact. Nonrational things happen: failures open doors, plans explode into insignificance, love diverts expectations, tragedies and losses alter life's picture, and serendipitous happenings surprise and bring change. Eventually individuals discover that seemingly small incidents create unexpected, dramatic, and major consequences.

Chasing the brass ring and pursuing goals can be bereft of fulfillment or satisfaction. Scratching another activity off a bucket list may empty the bucket, but it may also stymie the ability to find true meaning and purpose in life. In addition, living to fulfill someone else's expectations is pure lunacy, resulting in hollowness of spirit and accomplishment.

Living isn't driving through a flat and easy plain with no impasses or treacherous terrain. In life, pavement deteriorates, tires go flat, and gas runs low. How individuals got to where they are is not always the result of following a linear strategic map or a set of carefully chosen goals. Living is more complex than that, and getting lost is part of the deal. With age and perspective, the twisting road of life becomes clearer.

Frequently, chance or synchronicity is at work. Was it fate or luck or intention or divine intervention? Maybe destiny was present: the "daimon," according to psychologist James Hillman, that directs life and purpose and is sometimes referred to as a person's calling. People are unique, and that uniqueness calls them to follow their own course in their own way.

The book *Aging Well*, about the noted Harvard study of adult development, the longest longitudinal study of aging to date, describes the lives of three separate cohorts of 824 individuals over a span of 50 years. These individuals were selected during their teens and were a cross-section of the population and demographics. The study followed them for their entire lives and produced important information about the human life cycle and the factors that lead to a life of fulfillment.

George Vaillant states, "Positive aging means to love, to work, to learn something we did not know yesterday, and to enjoy the remaining precious moments with loved ones."[6] The study is important for understanding how individuals mature and progress to live a satisfying and rewarding life. Vaillant describes six "adult life tasks."[7]

In childhood, parents' perspectives and beliefs are accepted and mimicked. The last task of childhood is separation from the social, economic, residential, and ideological dependence on parents. Children learn to initiate their own activities and hopefully gain confidence and maturity and begin to move toward independence.

In adolescence, achieving a sense of identity is important, basically involving a "sense of one's own self, a sense of one's values, politics, and passions." Developing a personality and interests beyond the beliefs of one's parents or those of other individuals is a major development. Only when individuals gain a sense of their own identity can they move to the next stages.

Adolescents begin to realize their family's principles and create a set of personal values and goals that evolves into a coherent self-identity. This process occurs in other life stages as well, as events, challenges, controversies, and experience confront the values and principles of friends, society, and workplace.

Independence from parents is important, so individuals pursue a life and work that is fulfilling, enabling them to develop intimate friendships. Without creating a sense of self-identity, individuals are unable to achieve intimacy with others. To live with another person means "expanding one's sense of self to include another person."[8] Living in an interdependent, committed, and reciprocal relationship is important in adulthood, particularly in finding meaning.

A sense of self and intimacy are foundations for moving toward a broader landscape. Adulthood assumes a social identity, usually within the world of work. Work can include parenthood and the selfless care of children or others; it does not simply concern external employment. Work that involves a passion or mission increases meaning and satisfaction. Individuals desire a career that involves a commitment to important goals and purpose, along with compensation.

Individuals want to contribute, to give of themselves to ventures that are significant to them. Generativity involves giving of oneself unselfishly, which leads to providing leadership beyond one's own self-interest. Community building is involved. Simple kindness. Service. Caring for others. Concern for future generations. All move beyond selfish interests to an active concern for helping and guiding others. Generativity and integrity relate in part to meaning, or significance, and to a sense of wisdom and justice.

Adults later in life begin to come to terms with their decisions and how they resolved issues. In middle age, individuals begin to think about the next generation. Being a caring and understanding person extends to a future beyond the local community and embodies positive principles. Mentoring and teaching others are ways to ensure the maintenance of standards, which are the foundation for a life of integrity and wise decisions.

Wisdom is a virtue related to integrity and a spiritual sense of life—the spirit and heart—and a concern for social and world peace and order. Wisdom portrays common sense and moral judgment and the ability to understand the essence of issues and circumstances.

Character matters, in many cases more than accomplishments and titles do. Understanding that personal decisions made with integrity and adherence to principles and values are necessary to live an honorable and satisfying life, is essential. Whether an achievement is commendable or worthwhile is based on its foundational principles. Understanding that actions are admirable is more important than whether others agree with them. Principle produces a measure of integrity and virtue.

From a child's perspective, goodness always is to triumph and plans and rationality make up the absolute map for success. But it really doesn't always turn out that way: the unexpected occurs, what were thought of as truths were not, fairness doesn't always prevail, and rationality and human behavior are not always congruent. Understanding that society is a chaotic system that does not always operate rationally or by strict linear, scientific principles is necessary to comprehend events and forces.

In life, time is also a factor. While each minute is composed of sixty seconds and every hour sixty minutes, in reality, the minutes and hours do not seem to pass in equal increments. Sometimes, as the sayings go, time "drags" or it "flies." When happiness and closeness abound, time moves quickly. In times of distress and pain, the hands on the clock seem frozen.

Attitudes and feelings seem to sway the clock. Older people, as they look back, frequently cannot believe how fast their lives moved. They say, "It just seems like yesterday that . . . ," as they reflect and ponder their lives. Children experience time differently; holidays seem to arrive at a snail's pace, while time in the park passes in a wisp.

As people move through each stage of life, progress may not proceed at the pace they planned on, raising disbelief or anxiety or both. The fact of the matter is that in actuality people experience life in a metaphorical sense, like moving down a river in a canoe.

The river's current does not always move in consistent and equal measure as intended or desired. At times progress is made in expected intervals. Effort through work and paddling brings consistent progress. At other times, calm waters slow movement. Sometimes movement even stops, and progress seems nonexistent despite effort. Occasionally, the rapids move at a heart-pounding pace and the miles pass quickly. Each phase of the trip offers the opportunity for self-reflection and self-understanding. Self-discovery occurs in each phase, whether growth is slow but consistent, a sedentary period arises, or external conditions progress at a quick pace. In a sense, that's life.

Life is not always easy: valleys of disappointments and pain exist, but there are also peaks of satisfaction, joy, and connection. An individual's decisions have either positive or negative effects or both. Obstacles appear, some self-induced and others externally produced, but all are necessary to learn and contemplate what is important and what is trivial. Self-understanding will come from experience if reflection is part of the process.

Self-discovery and learning, however, come through success as well as hard times. Life does not always provide standing ovations, applause, or cheers. Self-expectation may not live up to personal performance, which can produce the corollary disappointment of not meeting one's standards or expectations.

Success or failure brings more decisions. The major one is how to react to circumstances. Some will learn from them and others may withdraw, becoming angry and pessimistic. Blaming others is a vacuous strategy that deflects responsibility in an effort to save a shallow self-concept. Success, if not viewed properly, can spur narcissistic self-adulation and disregard the work or support of others in the success.

The question a person must ask is, What is this experience trying to tell me? Learning from achievement or defeat can result in insight and self-discovery. The experiences also provide clarity into Who am I? and Why am I here?

Over the course of life, at any age, renewal is an option—a choice individuals make. Finding who we are also concerns examining the potential within. John Gardner stated, "Exploration of the full range of our potentialities is not something that we can safely leave to the chances of life. It is something to be pursued systematically, or at least avidly, to the end of our days. We should look forward to an endless and unpredictable dialogue between our potentialities and the claims of life—not only the claims we encounter but the claims we invent. And by potentialities I mean not just skills, but the full range of our capacities for sensing, wondering, learning, understanding, loving and aspiring."[9]

Everyone must confront fears and anxieties, otherwise they can be the barriers that imprison individuals from reaching out. Diversions and social distractions can impede any self-examination or self-knowledge. The courage to step forward, find contemplative space, and risk change is essential to growth and learning.

Watching eighteen-month-old toddlers is actually a lesson in human nature at its purest. The children are open: not confined by prejudices or opinions but just open to exploring and learning and finding the next new adventure. They experience joy at seeing birds and the amazement of smelling their first rose. They are open, unafraid of failure, and willing to get up again and try something new. They are constantly learning new things and reveling in the kisses and hugs of parents or grandparents. They experience life at its simplest, which comes with the gift of growth and learning.

In actuality, all lives, at every stage, should contain some of the same innocence and certainly the ongoing commitment and courage to rise up and learn. As individuals grow and mature, they look down the road, see what life holds and make decisions. In addition to the two basic questions everyone must face, other questions include: What are my obligations? What principles must I live up to? What are my true commitments? What are my talents and passions? What drives me? All these queries are essential for self-understanding and living, not simply existing, and for defining who one is.

Who You Are

Put away diplomas
Forget the titles
Bury your bank account
Hide your address.
What you are is not who you are.
What you are is too small for you to live.[10]
Who you are is greater than the positions you hold.
Who you are comes from the depths of your soul,
molded by those who love you,
and fired on a daily conflict of principle.
What you are fades into dust of death,
while your character arises from the grave, and
lives in the memories of men.

WHAT TO REMEMBER

- Physical characteristics are not reliable indicators of a person's self and character.
- Important aspects of life do not depend on strictly intelligent and physical prowess. Art, feelings, values, desire, and purpose are powerful directors of thought and action.

- The uniqueness of people is not always obvious from their physical image. Mind and heart and one's inner voice provide direction that is not always easily observed.
- Self-image and understanding develop from within as well as from external influences of family, society, and others.
- Fear is a potent force but not always a rational one. It can deter individual growth and development.
- Carpe diem: seize the day, move ahead, experience, learn from success and failure.
- Every circumstance provides an opportunity for renewal.

NOTES

1. Pruett, Kyle D., *Me, Myself, and I* (New York: Goddard Press, 1991), 10.

2. Emerson, Ralph Waldo, in *A Year with Emerson*, ed. Richard Grossman (Boston: David R. Godine Publisher, 2003), 34.

3. Whyte, David, *The Heart Aroused* (New York: Currency Doubleday 1994), 46.

4. Jobs, Steve, Commencement address, Stanford University, June 12, 2005, http://news.stanford.edu/2005/06/14/jobs-061505.

5. Schulman, Tom, screenwriter, *Dead Poets Society*, Touchstone Pictures, a Peter Weir Film, 1989.

6. Vaillant, George E., *Aging Well* (Boston: Little, Brown, and Company, 2002), 16.

7. Vaillant, *Aging Well*, 45–49.

8. Vaillant, *Aging Well*, 46.

9. Gardner, John W., *Self Renewal: The Individual and the Innovative Society* (New York: W. W. Norton and Company, 1995), 11.

10. Inspired by David Whyte, "What to Remember When Waking."

2

LONGING, BELONGING, AND GROWTH

There is meaning in every journey that is unknown to the traveler.
—Dietrich Bonhoeffer

It is beneath human dignity to lose one's individuality and become a mere cog in the machine.
—Mahatma Gandhi

Newborn children come into this world with a great aura of innocence and possibility. Parents, grandparents, friends, and neighbors wonder what will become of this new life. Gender, race, ethnicity, or any other demographic does not really matter; the hopes are the same for all: health, happiness, and a good life.

Mystery surrounds the children as well. Certainly there are genetic dispositions that influence their appearance and other less visible characteristics. However, personality, character, and a sense of self-awareness also affect perspective and passion and growth and development, in addition to environment, experiences, relationships, and mentors.

The child's path throughout life is unknown and to be determined. Love and a sense of security are important. Parenting and experience are essential as children develop attitudes and learn values. Even in the preschool years, children learn important values that can set a foundation for their future. For example, honesty and truthfulness, as well as a sense of justice and treating others with consideration, are important to learn. Developing determination and understanding responsibilities when facing challenges are also essential throughout their lives.

Values and principles undergird perspective and personality. While everyone's physical body parts are the same—heart, organs, and muscles—their selves and personalities differ. Society and relationships influence a person's attitudes and disposition, through personal and individual encounters and challenges.

What interests and stimulates and what bores and deflates individuals differ for each person. Everyone is destined to have accomplishments and disappointments. Social pressure plays a significant role in influencing how individuals perceive and feel about themselves, especially in younger years.

In a nutshell, each person is a complex being that includes not only a body but also a mind, heart, and soul, which are affected by tangible and intangible influences. Together they create a distinctive and critically important self.

Tom Stoppard's play, *The Hard Problem*, discusses the issues of brain and mind and illustrates the differences. The protagonist Hilary states, "Who's the you outside your brain? Where?"[1] In Hilary's discussion with Spike about consciousness, he states that with consciousness there is a "mind-body problem." He says, "The body is made of things and things don't have thoughts."[2] The mind is immune to X-rays or photos and exists inside a person, directing thought and behavior. It is not always predictable.

The developing mind is only seen in attitudes and behavior; as an unobservable entity, it cannot be viewed or touched. Surgeons do brain surgery, but the mind is intangible and nowhere to be found because it involves consciousness, thinking, memory, and judgment.

Parents have an obvious and ongoing impact on children discovering who they are and what their views of life are. It goes without saying that parents live a bit within each child throughout their lives, whether parents were positive or negative, functional or dysfunctional models. If a parent dies or is absent, the absence is an influence on the child's self-identity and perspective throughout life. The absence of a parent is present throughout life, even into maturity.

MIND AND HEART

All parents want their children to grow into independent and competent people who can fulfill the promise that lives within them. To do so requires the development of mind, body, heart, and spirit. Character and self-understanding are critically important in becoming a mature adult.

The mind involves intellectual and mental faculty for applying reason, perspective, and memory. All are necessary for understanding and confronting life's complexities and multifaceted social, scientific, and political issues. Logic, analysis, and ethical comprehension are important in these circumstances.

People, however, are not just made up of intellect. Contrary to technology operating solely on artificial linear and binary intelligence, people have feelings, requiring an understanding of matters of the heart. The emotions of love, compassion, sadness, and happiness, among others, when connected with mind, create responses and actions to situations and conditions.

Emotions are sparked by events, and events are sparked by emotions. Clarity of circumstances is not always evident when the mind says one thing and the heart pleads for another. Logic and emotion are not always on the same page. The question of whether mind or heart controls actions is dependent on each person's sense of self: logic sometimes conflicts with emotion and vice versa. These circumstances can cause confusion and anxiety as to what to follow; should it be emotion or logic? Occasionally, individuals may state, "This seems like the best course, but it doesn't feel right." How individuals think and respond to emotions is a part of their personality and temperament.

LONGING AND BELONGING

With matters of the heart come desires and needs. Poet John O'Donohue wrote,

> Every human heart is full of longing. You want to be happy, to live a meaningful and honest life, to find love, and to be able to open your heart to someone; you long to discover who you are and to learn how to heal your own suffering and become free and compassionate. To

be alive is to be suffused with longing. The voices of longing keep your life alert and urgent. If you cannot discover the shelter of belonging within your life you'll become a victim and target of your longing, pulled hither and thither without any anchorage anywhere."[3]

Times exist when individuals yearn for change because they do not feel they belong or are connected, that they are not a good fit for the circumstances or work. Their heart is not "in it," and fulfillment is absent. This occurs even when compensation, prestige, or success is present and ample.

People yearn to belong, to define the path from isolation to connection. Inside everyone's soul is the means to true relationship with others and nature. Everyone needs a sense of belonging, which is a matter of heart: it is a feeling, a sense. Each person's experience is not fully accessible to others; others may observe a person and that person's circumstances but not experience the passion or feeling the person feels and confronts in those circumstances. Feelings are not always portrayed in physical behavior: sometimes individuals cloak their inner thoughts and emotions, such as hurt and anger, in silence and stillness.

Compassion opens the possibility of connection. People sense the impact of events on others because they themselves lived them or because they can put themselves in the place of others. Sensing another person's overt or covert reactions takes an awareness of the subtleties of emotion. A feeling of community is a sense that everyone is connected to each other. Too often society separates people by gender, race, ethnicity, or some other category when in fact they are all just human beings.

Each person—each soul—longs for relationship. Without a sense of belonging and connection, all achievements, status, and possessions seem empty and futile. The anchor of life is a sense of belonging where heart and mind envelop the virtues of truth, goodness, justice, unity, and love. A sense of understanding and warmth comes with mind and heart and an attachment beyond the formality of rules and duties. Heart and soul can traverse events and circumstances and foster an understanding beyond pure reason.

EARLY CHILDHOOD

Early childhood is very important because all aspects of a child's "competence, personality, and temperament are being set."[4] What parents do not realize is that this period of a child's life is extremely critical "for now and a lifetime."

Children experience enormous brain growth in their first three years. According to Kyle Pruett, developmental researchers have proven the "remarkable" effects of early care and enhancing cognitive growth and learning ability. Quality childcare at this stage affects cognitive learning but also social skills, responsiveness, and emotional control and expression.

Adults sometimes think these early years are fairly inconsequential except for physical growth and dexterity. Many parents, by choice or need, rely on others for their toddler's care. Pruett states, "The self—the ME—of the young child emerges in this 18-month era with such force that it feels more like a geologic event than a stage in development. After months and months of figuring out what is me and *not* me in the world, children are so anxious to put this new understanding to a test that we, as parents, often feel that all we can do is direct traffic."[5]

Children at this age demonstrate tremendous vitality and desire to find what they are about. Exploring and curiosity are off the charts. Fear of failure or others' expectations are not evident to them. Energy and inquisitiveness are major parts of their waking hours: they are watching, learning, and doing.

Relationships with parents and others "are what make our young human."[6] Creating trusting relationships nurture young children and build an inner feeling of emotional strength. Toddlers begin to distinguish between "me" and "not-me," leading to "mine" and "not mine."

Children's growth in these years sets a foundation for the future and how children feel and behave. Experiences and encounters with parents are important. Their feelings and moods are as significant as their doings. Emotions are openings to the heart and spirit as well as thinking and learning. All of this is of consequence because success in life depends on cognition and problem solving, social skills, and a sense of emotional security and understanding.

PASSAGE TO MATURITY

During the critical first six years, children begin to lay the foundation for personality and character development. They learn from adults as well as from their own positive and negative experiences. With appropriate parental and adult security, they come to like themselves and others, and they are keen observers who emulate what they see in the actions of parents and others.

Elmore defines several phases beyond early childhood in moving to maturity.[7] The second phase, ages six to twelve, focuses on formulation of character. Children choose models and identify with "heroes": they think about the lives of those whom they admire. Values develop and they begin to understand value judgments, social awareness, and connections with others. The need for compliance to authority becomes clearer, and they build skills to understand what is and what is not important.

A third phase involves ages thirteen to twenty, in which children begin to create who they will become as adults, observing and evaluating others for their style to determine whether or not it fits with their manner and image. Socialization is the means by which to do this, and as parents know, adolescents also push back on their values and become more independent. This is a period of testing and social awareness.

Greater discretion and independence require growth in personal discipline. Making decisions that meet standards of appropriate conduct is necessary because parental or other supervision is not always available. With greater understanding comes greater responsibility and accountability. Accountability—social, legal, and personal—is necessary as independence expands.

A more realistic conceptualization of life and its possibilities must be established. Self-esteem certainly is important, as are healthy social relationships and peer groups. In addition, they begin to see beyond the tangible world and grow spiritually. Beliefs become clear and others' values, when contemplated, become issues for deliberation, debate, and discussion.

Young adults in their twenties and thirties grow and learn through application, not strictly through instruction. They actually do what they know. Interpersonal skills such as conflict resolution, listening, and forgiving are gained by and through experience. They begin to conceptualize reality and understand how society works beyond childhood myths and Hollywood fiction. Past perceptions are challenged, and new perspectives emerge as experience and relationships expand.

In addition, individuals demonstrate loyalty and submit to leaders through belief in a cause. Greater clarity of their longer-term vision and future develops as they gain greater understanding of their skills, talents, and strengths. They also begin to cultivate empathy and relationship skills and realize their influence and impact in relationships with others.

The next five to twelve years—midlife—bear some of the fruit of individuals' past labors. They gain a tighter focus on their "being" as well as their "doings," as they reap the tangible and personal rewards of work and relationships. While external "doings" are important, they also look inward, to their inner life and needs, and formulate a more definitive picture of what they believe and stand for.

The purpose and mission of life become clearer. Priorities and motives sharpen, and productivity and leadership produce results and greater influence. As all this is taking place, those at the midlife stage are willing to sacrifice because they are a part of something larger than themselves.

In this phase "who we are, what we do, and where we do it converge as a reward."[8] Career is a period of momentum, effectiveness, broad vision, and generosity. Some individuals never experience this phase because of complacency, financial obsession, false priorities, or self-defeating behavior. Loving life is a part of this phase, and relationships with others are an important priority. Individuals move into this stage through attitude adjustments, retooling their skills, or a change of heart. Wisdom is demonstrated, which is sought out by others.

The elder phase brings an "afterglow" in which a sense of fulfillment, calm presence, and authority are present in people's lives. People actively seek out these qualities, and their range of influence widens. As individuals grow and find that "know thyself" is coming true for them, they have emotional intelligence, a sense of ethics, a focus on what's truly important, and an understanding of their strengths. They provide leadership and think beyond themselves in serving others and valuing community.

SOCIETY AND RELATIONSHIPS

Self-concept is not developed in isolation. The question "Who am I?" has rudiments in family life and interactions with parents and others. Contacts and social interactions with adults as well as peers are important in both small and sometimes major ways. The effect of acceptance, rejection, or indifference can be profound.

When adolescents, for example, ask, "Who am I?" their answer frequently depends on the feedback they received from the world around them and their peers. Their fears are a huge influence. How other people see them affects how they perceive themselves. Teachers' actions and reactions, along with those of relatives, neighbors, or employers are notable.

Social interactions raise questions about personal self-concept. Any middle or high school teacher will attest to the power of peers on students' attitudes, feelings, beliefs, hopes, and viewpoints from friends, mentors, and role models. Actually, in adult life, there are similar influences on opinions and self-perspective. Cooperation or competition, connection or isolation, conformity or independence, confidence or doubt can be at play, each creating moments of significance and decision-making.

Individuals, both children and adults, desire to have others perceive them positively, but positive self-esteem alone does not always make the individual perform to high levels. Issues of authenticity and integrity are also important. Some individuals have a confident, positive self-concept, while others do not feel good about themselves and shy away from anything that will expose it. Authenticity, at times, takes courage.

An individual's desire to be perceived positively can lead to seeking a means to enhance social status and present a favorable image to others. This occurs in both childhood and adulthood. Roles become important and stature matters, and, sometimes, individuals are not genuine because of social or political pressure. People hide their true selves behind a façade of posturing, roles, and image.

Most people do not live in isolation: they need connection with others from childhood through adulthood. Individuals engage in associations, groups, and social settings that have a variety of influences. Those who are part of that social life depends, in part, on schedules and finances as well as a person's political, economic, educational, social, and professional background.

In these relationships, individuals test themselves, and these encounters influence their inner life. Conflicts arise at times between the individual, on the one hand, and social expectations and relationships, on the other. Disagreements spur clashes between the individual and the norms of the group. Pressure and conflict occur internally from the individual's self-image and beliefs contrasted with social perceptions.

Peer groups play an important role because of their influence on values, appearance, and conduct. The focus on ideas and issues becomes a part of peer commitments and demands. For many individuals, standing alone away from the group is demanding because of the fear of ostracism. The need to belong is great. Who wants to be an outcast? Standing alone on principle is difficult at any age when social acceptance is at stake. It takes courage.

The pressure to conform can be suffocating. Sometimes parents want their son or daughter to comply with certain ideals and images: being funny, beautiful, talented, smart, or sociable. Certainly the media and marketers push conformity in appearance and dress. Being different is not what society or commercial business desires. There are products to sell! Images to maintain! Commercialism thrives!

Madison Avenue and marketers continue to rant, "You need these clothes to look good; you need a ton of friends to be happy; money will make you happy; you need this body to look fit; being popular means you are respected, and you will be part of the group if you just. . . ." All of this contrasts and conflicts with the national axiom, "American individualism."

Social pressure can be immense and produce compliance. Relationships enhance lives significantly, but if they require conformity or questionable behavior, they can be psychologically difficult and dubious. Peer pressure can drive individuals to do questionable or unethical things because of these relationships. However, "the outcome of ethical relationships is the development of a self that is more than the sum of those interactions—what some refer to as the 'real' you, your inner or private self."[9]

SOCIAL PRESSURE

Social pressure can alter an individual's picture of reality. Fitting in becomes very important, and sometimes, good sense becomes the victim. This is true for adults as well as children and adolescents. Close-knit groups are very powerful and create pressure to comply. If you don't comply, you're out.

Society's expectations are influential but are not always the same for men and women. A Pew research study (2017) found that the American public has different views of what it values in males versus females. [10] For men, the traits or characteristics most valued include:

Honesty/morality	33 percent
Professional/financial success	23 percent
Ambition/leadership	19 percent
Strength/toughness	19 percent
Hard work/work ethic	18 percent

When it comes to women, what society values most includes:

Physical attractiveness	35 percent
Intelligence	22 percent
Honesty/morality	14 percent
Ambition/leadership	9 percent
Professional/financial success	8 percent

An interesting finding is that politeness/respectfulness garnered only 5 percent as a valued trait for both men and women. So much for civility. Physical attractiveness has little, if anything, to do with character or integrity. To be judged simply by one's physical attractiveness does not necessarily correlate with a person's internal self, integrity, and disposition.

These traits defined by the general public are indications of social perspectives, prejudices, and expectations about both genders. Some of the qualities are similar for both: honesty/morality, ambition/leadership, and professional/financial success. Several others diverge on the basis of gender, for example, hard work/work ethic for men and physical attractiveness for women.

Adults at work and in the community are pressured to demonstrate socially acceptable traits. In the business or professional worlds, one would think that the attractiveness of physical appearance would not be a big or major factor. Honesty and morality, politeness and respectfulness, and leadership and ambition are in tune with a person's self-image and character.

Today's adolescents spend a great deal of time on social media. In another study, Pew examined the views of teens aged thirteen to seventeen, on social media and their effect on people their age.[11] On the positive side, teens indicated that social media helps them to:

Connect with friends/family	40 percent
Finding news/information easily	16 percent
Meet those with same interests	15 percent
Stay entertained/upbeat	9 percent

On the negative side, social media promotes:

Bullying/rumor spreading	27 percent
Harm to relationships/lack of in-person contact	17 percent
Unrealistic views of others' lives	15 percent
Distractions/addictions	14 percent
Peer pressure	12 percent

When examining the impact of peer group pressure, both anonymous and person-specific, social media is a very powerful force on teens and young adults. These pressures are difficult for anyone to contend with, let alone thirteen- to seventeen-year-olds. Individuals can reel under social media attacks and taunts. The truth gets twisted or total fabrications are presented, and they are difficult to refute or correct.

The PBS *Frontline* series produced a program on the effect of the internet on young people entitled "Generation Like."[12] Douglas Rushkoff stated on camera, "Likes, follows, friends, retweets—they're the social currency of this generation, 'Generation Like.' The more likes you have, the better you feel."

Will, a high school student, replied, "You can't wait to find out whether people like you or not, so you need likes and stuff like that, instant gratification." The *Frontline* program emphasized the fact that students, through the internet, want recognition and fame based on the number of "likes" they receive.

Our society exalts celebrity. Narcissism reigns. Children are exposed to this ad nauseam. The media and technology proclaim individuals' success and virtue based on wealth, having a picture on a magazine cover each month, and the overemphasis on sports and entertainment as the means to popularity, fiscal security, and importance. But in reality, as suicides and substance abuse demonstrate, celebrity can mask deeper issues. Fame may bring fortune and tangibles but leave the soul and heart empty.

Falling prey to distractions and excuses sidetrack individuals from pursuing a purposeful path. It is always easier to hook into another episode of Hollywood fluff or let the Xbox's (ugh!) seduction take control. Self-control is essential in today's world with all of its distractions and social "noise." To reach one's goals takes more than ambition; it requires self-control to steer the course.

Trivia and continuous streams of entertainment and diversion actually detach people from each other and stop them from pursuing their purpose. Wisdom is not even a consideration, nor can it be nurtured, when individuals are controlled by their devices. The self gets lost in the cacophony of technological babble. Decadence can fester in this environment through lost standards, ethics, or moral sensibility.

A sense of self involves mind, heart, and soul. The pressures of life—peer, family, self—can create a false direction. Poets bring the nonmetric and authentic aspects of an individual's inner life, voice, and self-image to light. The longing to belong is a powerful personal force. Not all motivations come from aspirations or desires.

> The invisible is one of the huge regions in your life. Some of the most important things about you and your life are invisible. What you think and the way you think control how you feel, how you meet people, and how you see the world. Yet your thoughts are invisible. One of the most fascinating questions about your thinking is, Why do you have the thoughts that you do, and why do you link them together in these patterns? The secret bridges from thought to thought are invisible. No surgeon operating on a brain has ever found a crevice full of thoughts. What you believe about yourself determines how

people treat you. You can never see your beliefs. Belief is invisible. Your feelings make you sad or happy, yet feelings are visible too. [13]

The Gordian Knot

Across the valley of time I lost my way
Trudging through each day in heavy shoes
Of doubt about a life without virtue,
Punctuated with hidden dreams and
Lost in the manipulation of the Gordian knot.
Can I be who I am? Or
Must I don the cloak of deception,
A Chameleon's misty garb, that burns
Thin from the flames of acceptance.

WHAT TO REMEMBER

- Sometimes logic and emotion conflict. Both rationality and emotion affect decisions.
- People yearn to belong, to define a path away from isolation to connection.
- Early childhood is an extremely important time as children's "competence, personality, and temperament" are being set. These years establish a foundation for the future.
- Self-concept is not developed in isolation. Individuals desire to be perceived positively. The need to belong is great.
- Social pressure can alter a person's view of reality. It can be immense and produce compliance, which can be detrimental in terms of a person's individuality.
- Self-control is essential for continued growth and learning as well as for becoming self-reflective.
- A sense of self involves the mind, heart, and soul.

NOTES

1. Stoppard, Tom. *The Hard Problem* (New York: Grove Press, 2015), 1026.
2. Stoppard, *Hard Problem*, 267.

3. O'Donohue, John, *Eternal Echoes* (New York: HarperCollins, 1999), 7.

4. Pruett, Kyle D., *Me, Myself, and I* (New York: Goddard Press, 1999), 3.

5. Pruett, *Me, Myself, and I*, 52.

6. Pruett, *Me, Myself, and I*, 4.

7. Elmore, Tim, *Artificial Maturity* (San Francisco: Jossey-Bass Publishers, 2012), 205–12.

8. Elmore, *Artificial Maturity*, 211.

9. Dobrin, Arthur, "The Astonishing Power of Social Pressure," *Psychology Today*, April 14, 2014, https://www.psychologytoday.com/us/experts/arthur-dobrin-dsw.

10. Pew Research Center, "Americans See Different Expectations for Men and Women," http://www.pewsocialtrends.org/2017/12/05/americans-see-different-expectations-for-men-and-women/.

11. Pew Research Center, "Teens, Social Media and Technology 2018," http://www.pewinternet.org/2018/05/31/teens-social-media-technology-2018/.

12. *Frontline*, "Generation Like," https://www.pbs.org/wgbh/frontline/film/generation-like/.

13. O'Donohue, *Eternal Echoes*, 27.

3

LOOKING BEYOND THE COVER

It is only when one feels joy or sorrow that one knows anything about himself, and only by joy or sorrow is he instructed what to seek and what to shun.

—Goethe

Death is not the greatest loss in life. The greatest loss is what dies inside of us while we live.

—Norman Cousins

Bookstores have a multitude of books, with unique covers that entice customers over to look at and buy them. That's the ploy: alluring covers and images stimulate interest and popularity. However, the old axiom "Don't judge a book by its cover" applies not only to books but also to people.

A book's cover may attract one person but deflect others. Enticing covers do not tell the whole story. There may be three, four, or more themes and stories buried beneath the outer cover. The same is true for people: much more is there than is evident to the outer eye.

Prejudices about external appearance create false impressions and expectations that may have nothing to do with the person as a human being. People should not be judged on their appearance or surface characteristics. Getting to know someone and seeing what is inside may give an entirely different perspective on the person's qualities or depth.

WHAT'S GOING ON?

A lot is going on within each person. Each page of someone's life documents struggles, successes, failures, victories, joy, creativity, pain, doubts, losses, and gains. A life story frequently moves in a nonlinear, unplanned manner and inconsistent time frame; it is complex and filled with emotion and relationships. Decisions do not always meet standards of common sense and reason. Perspectives develop and learning occurs as values and principles are challenged and tested internally or externally.

The human mind and soul are not visibly tangible. They are reflected only in attitudes and behavior and emerge through mindsets and viewpoints that are the foundation of decisions and actions. An individual's values, principles, and ethics can be seen only in decisions and their wisdom and impact. As the old saying goes, "Actions speak louder than words"—and louder than, as might be added, physical appearance.

A person's internal view of self may be quite different from how others might describe him or her. Self-image is a product of one's earlier life as a child, encounters and impressions from adolescence to adulthood, and the trials and tribulations of life overall. Values evolve as perspectives deviate from the past. What one used to believe can fade into the past, and self-image adjusts accordingly. Over time, self-identity may change, because knowledge and experiences, coupled with self-reflection, transform who one is and who one desires to be.

Life and being, at times, are not always transparent and clear; they can be abstract and opaque. Certainly there are tangibles, but there are also ethereal—graceful and fragile—aspects of life that move in a more poetic and idiosyncratic manner than in a technical one. Small and unanticipated changes create divergent and sometimes major unexpected outcomes. The beauty of life comes in creative sparks and intuition that find pathways not always taken. The road less traveled may be the most enticing and productive.

People desire to live lives of significance and meaning, and hopefully wisdom, which move far beyond data and statistics. The things people desire internally are difficult to quantify. Noble ideas nourish the heart and soul, fueling one's passion to discover and serve something greater than self-interest. Creativity sparks internally and brings perspective not seen by others. Love moves people beyond logic and self-regard.

Sometimes seemingly insignificant factors effect major changes. Data, algorithms, or philosophical projections cannot always predict one's life. The idea that one minor change can alter outcomes also applies to individuals. The stock market, society, and weather are examples of nonlinear systems that are not always predictable and can bring about dramatic changes. Life is also not always predictable; sometimes chance meetings or unexpected events dramatically alter people's lives. A child's life is not a precursor to the events and outcomes of the child's adult life.

People scrutinize data and information, but their desires and needs are more abstract and ethereal. Data becomes information, which provides knowledge, and hopefully, knowledge will create understanding from which insight and wisdom emanate. But this is not always the case: many highly intelligent people have done bright and creative as well as stupid and evil things. Desires are not always rational and can override reason and ethics.

Knowledge, however, requires perspective and critical and complex thinking in order to fully understand issues and context as well as to distinguish between truth and opinion or speculation. In addition, applying knowledge involves considering values and principles, without which goodness, integrity, and honor would be absent.

Knowing means connecting the head with the heart and sensing what to act on and when to do it. Time is a factor in many decisions. Frequently judgments have to be made without hard, analytical data because it is not relevant or not available in a timely manner. In addition, unseen forces at play can affect options and conclusions.

People with a deep knowledge of their true self and circumstances understand things without formal analysis and make the intuitive choices necessary to achieve results. Intuition involves the heart and spirit. Even when facts and knowledge are not available, and logic and reasoning are confined, individuals get an intuitive sense of right and wrong and what to do.

At times, intuition causes individuals to go against the grain of expectation and tradition. Significant relationships serve something greater than personal interests. Living is about "being" present and aware. Meister Eckhart, the German theologian, stated, "People should not consider as much about what they do but rather about what they are. If they and their ways are good, then their deeds are radiant. If you are righteous, then what you do will also be righteous"[1] Eckhart was speaking theologically, but this also applies to everyone who acts out of honorable and moral purpose. Within each person are principled desires that can spur courageous action.

"Being" has to do with authenticity and the uniqueness of each individual, founded in inner values, beliefs, integrity, and humor. Primarily it has to do with the nature of human relationships and a person's moral and ethical core in facing and creating a life. With that, at times, come pressure and even tears. Individuals secure in their being take risks, endure criticism in hard times, and do not bow to the attachments of power or possessions.

DISCOVERING SELF

According to Carl Rogers, individuals with high self-worth have confidence and positive feelings about themselves and are open to other people, not closed off or reticent with others.[2] They face challenges and accept that failures and unhappiness occur at times.

On the other hand, individuals with low self-worth are defensive and guarded with other people and avoid challenges for fear of failing and slumping into difficult times. They do not feel good or confident about themselves and consequently do not stretch their capabilities or talents. They are close-minded.

Finding a sense of self may require taking several routes, according to Rogers. Some individuals move away from exposing who they really are, basically defining who they are negatively. The fear is that others may not find their real nature interesting and appealing, so they do not share who they really are. Being fearful, they hide behind a façade because of the little regard they have for themselves.

Other individuals move away from "oughts": the compelling images of who they "ought to be." The "oughts" may come from parents or others about how and what their lives "ought" to be, that is, how they should live and what they should do. These individuals reject the perceptions of others with regard to their lives and what they should pursue.

Meeting the expectations of others also emanates from what the social or corporate culture expects, for example, the "organization man." By being a member of a group, the individual subordinates individuality for group compliance and acceptance, and identity shifts from self to a group. Group expectations and values exceed personal or creative ones; group, not individual, viewpoints dominate.

People also have individualized perspectives that differ from those of others. An individual who tells himself or herself, "This is what I should do" is rejecting what others think. Such individuals look beyond the expectations of others and are true to themselves, pushing away conformity and exercising their individual freedom and resourcefulness to do what they feel is best. What others desire is rejected, along with social and peer pressure to meet expectations of the group.

Individualism prevails, not uniformity or compliance. Finding a sense of self can create conflicts with others' speculation. Self-direction and individual responsibility have an inner focus that collide with the ideas and values of others.

Self-acceptance of internal change is required to find a sense of self. People must trust themselves and the values that are integral to them. Growing into maturity requires moving away from pleasing others, from meeting others' preferences, or from fearing rejection by others. The individual "finds himself increasingly willing to be, with greater accuracy and depth, that self which he most truly is."[3]

Individuals with a high sense of self-esteem are more likely to have well-articulated views of self. They understand their strengths and weaknesses, their stance on values and principles, and their ability to raise and assess issues. Whereas those with low self-esteem have inconsistent, uncertain, and unstable views of themselves. High levels of self-concept clarity result in lower levels of depression, anxiety, neuroticism, and stress. They also result in the ability to take action, view situations in a more positive way, and interact with people more freely.

WANTS AND NEEDS

When growing up, all people face the pressures of wants and needs. In many cases, they cannot distinguish between them, but the difference is quite simple.

Needs include the fundamentals for living: food, water, shelter, security, and health care. Everyone requires them to survive. Wants, on the other hand, are things people desire or fancy. They may be things the individual may or may not be able to obtain and generally are tied to hopes and dreams. Wants are not necessities.

Parents ensure that their children's needs are provided for; that is a basic responsibility for parents, and it may extend to caretakers, teachers, friends, and others. In cases where there are lapses because of family dysfunction or economic or other turmoil, such a stabilizing factor as caring for children's needs may be weakened or missing.

On the other hand, some parents "helicopter," hovering over their children for fear that the children's basic needs or desires are threatened. Others may "snowplow," clearing the way of conflict, challenges, responsibilities, or external requirements and demands for their children. Children in these cases are perceived not to be responsible for their behavior or circumstances. Parental "helicoptering" and "snowplowing" stem from a distorted view of successful parenting. Children must learn to deal with circumstances, particularly those of their own making.

Parents meet the basic needs of young children, but when it comes to wants, they may deny them. A child's wanting something—a bike or technology or something else—may be rejected because of cost, principle, or philosophy. Children may want something for a variety of reasons: friends may have it, it's faddish, or it's a matter of stature or egotism. There may not be much motivation for wanting something other than to gain acceptance or validation.

As children grow, so do the number of wants. "They [i.e., wants] become more diverse, more complex, though no less compelling. As children are exposed to broadening circles of influence, the legitimation of wants and needs falls increasingly to teachers, peers, clergy, media, employers, government, and ultimately to society. Needs are social, and the conflicts over their legitimacy, their meaning, their extent, their satisfaction, take political form."[4]

Conflict between needs and wants exists in many phases of life. Needs may change as experience, talent, and skills are developed and refined. A young person may be satisfied with an entry-level position and compensation, but that satisfaction may decrease as individual experience is gained and a promotion or change to more complex work is "needed." In addition, the need for recognition increases: sitting in the back row is no longer satisfying or acceptable.

Abraham Maslow's notable needs hierarchy published in 1943, *A Theory of Human Motivation*, identifies five levels of needs: physical, security, social, ego, and self-actualization. Two levels—physical and security—have to do with the basic human needs. Social needs include belonging, love, and inclusion, and ego comprises such aspects as self-esteem, recognition, power, and prestige. When individuals satisfy their physical needs, they turn to social and ego needs. Hunger, security, or safety requirements, when not fulfilled, are impediments to growth and the ability to reach one's potential.

Not everyone achieves the fifth level, a sense of self-actualization, whereas the other four levels can be met as their deficiencies drive individuals to grow and meet them. Self-actualization involves finding meaning in life and fully meeting one's potential. To do so, one must put life in perspective and self-actualize through awareness, objectivity, creativity, honesty, and independence. And to do this, one must meet lower needs or be willing to step off the safest and expected path of conformity, risking failure and rejection. Trying to fulfill others' expectations is a dead-end road to achieving self-actualization.

In actuality, both parents and individuals desire similar things from life. Parents want their children to grow up confident and secure and find adventure and enjoyment. When confronted with issues and problems, they want them to be able to face and resolve them. While parents want their offspring to find happiness that leads to a good life, finding satisfaction and meaning are precursors that ultimately bring happiness.

Generally, adolescents and young adults want similar things. The parenting they experience is important in how they confront and approach life. Childhoods—happy or difficult—affect attitudes, temperament, perspectives, and self-understanding. Sometimes fate intervenes and alters the traditional path. Parenting greatly affects "the way your child's temperament is shaped for the long-term."[5]

PARENTS LOST

What if the major influence of one or both parents is lost? The absence of a parent has intense and long-lasting effects. What happens to children's development of self, temperament, and security and safety needs when they suffer the death or loss of a parent? C. S. Lewis stated, "With my mother's death all settled happiness, all that was tranquil and reliable, disappeared from my life. There was to be much fun, many pleasures, many stabs at joy; but no more of the old security. It was sea and islands now; the great continent had sunk like Atlantis."[6]

Facing an unexpected death, for example, particularly for children who lose a parent is excruciating, especially at an early age. When she was four years old, Claire Bower's mother died of complications during childbirth. In an essay from a speech she gave in 2016 for Every Mother Counts, a nonprofit initiated by Christy Turlington and dedicated to making childbirth safer, Claire stated,

> Growing up was hard, there is no possible way to sugar coat that; I would be lying if I said it was easy.
>
> When I was growing up I would often try to suppress my own emotions simply so that I would feel strong and like I had accomplished something, when truly, ignoring the reality of my emotions and failing to face them head on accomplished absolutely nothing but prolonged heartache. Learning to face the emotions, the heartache, and the loss was a day to day learning process but one that to this day has made me who I am.
>
> Moreover, it taught me that through hardships we must find courage, confront our own emotions, grow wiser through experience, and learn to cope with the situation so that we do not live the rest of our lives dwelling within a shadow of loss. These lessons have made me strong and have given me a much different perspective of the concept of life, along with its purpose.
>
> Growing up without my biological mother was not easy, but it did teach me something. I cannot change what has happened to me, but I can take the negative things that have happened in the past 16 years, and I can consciously choose to use them to make a positive impact and find a purpose. If using my story and what I have learned from my experience to spread awareness can help one person, it has helped somebody, and I have served a purpose. That is what is now important to me.
>
> At the end of your life will you be proud of what you did and who you impacted? That is what we should all be asking ourselves. So let's all step out, find our purpose, and fulfill it.[7]

Circumstances like these are defining moments that exist throughout life. This speech from a then sixteen-year-old demonstrates wisdom, maturity, and fortitude—rising up and not adopting a victim mentality. People, even young ones, can decide how they are going to react to situations, including heartbreaking ones. That decision cannot be taken away by anyone: each person has total freedom and control in determining his or her response.

A sense of rootlessness is created when a child, who is unclear as to who he or she is, confronts the loss of a security anchor—a parent and/or a major role model. When the model is gone, some children feel a sense of responsibility for it or resort to a strong attitude of independence. An ongoing sense of wondering how life would be different if the parent had lived exists throughout life and even into old age.

Absent a parental model, the child creates the "self in a vacuum." Harris states, "The fundamental task of every man and woman is to create the self. How do we take the raw material of childhood and turn it into a cohesive adult self? More than in probably any other task, a child feels the loss of a parent in this daunting assignment. A parent, especially the same-sexed parent—a father for a boy and a mother for girl—serves as a living example of how to be a person. The loss of that parent leaves the child frighteningly alone."[8]

Parents set the example for children for how to be a person. They learn "by taking that example, trying it on for a time, discarding the elements that do not fit, perhaps even tearing it to shreds before we can arrive at a sense of self that feels personally meaningful and authentic."[9] Parents, relatives, role models, and others affect the development of self. While others may influence, only the individual can find the path to self-identity.

Philosopher Friedrich Nietzsche discussed the impact of finding oneself. He stated, "No one can build you the bridge on which you, and only you, must cross the river of life. There may be countless trails and bridges and demigods who would gladly carry you across; but only at the price of pawning and forgoing yourself. There is one path in the world that none can walk but you. Where does it lead? Don't ask, walk!"[10] Not an easy task.

He suggests looking inside and asking several questions: "What have you truly loved thus far? What has ever uplifted your soul, what has dominated and delighted it at the same time?"[11] By answering these questions, people may find the fundamental law of their true selves.

Not all people have a clear sense of who they are; their status and where they are going in life is not clear. Certainly many adolescents are in this frame of mind, but it is also true for many adults. Looking inward is not easy and requires solitude and introspection.

SELF AND TECHNOLOGY

Sometimes the tools that are available distract people from facing major questions. With so much emphasis on technology today, it is easy to think that it can hold the answer to direction and contentment in one's life. Just follow the data and prescribed procedures and a good life will unfold.

Dee Hock, the father of the universal Visa credit card, said, "We're now at the point in time when the ability to receive, utilize, store, transform, and transmit data—the lowest cognitive form—has expanded literally beyond comprehension. Understanding and wisdom are largely forgotten as we struggle under an avalanche of data and information. In the ever-accelerating assault of data and information on cognitive capacity, understanding and wisdom may be declining in absolute as well as relative terms."[12]

While technology offers many things, it certainly provides distraction. People—children and adults—put their nose into the screen and distract themselves from the people and events around them. Is a virtual-reality sunset better than looking up and seeing and experiencing nature in front of one's own eyes? Can technology really replace mentors and polestars?

People avoid the reality of life by consuming time with virtual reality. Being absent, not present in real time with real people seems psychotic. Seeing the Grand Canyon virtually, through someone else's outlook, removes any personal perspective, emotion, or imagination. Virtual technology is a computer-generated simulation or three-dimensional image that can be interacted with in a seemingly real manner. Real life, however, has greater possibilities that are not reflected in computer-coded choices and directions. Seeing a picture or film of a loved one is far different than experiencing their real presence.

Technology lays information and "contactability" ("connection" is stretching it) at society's disposal. But it also sidetracks people from the present and from the feelings, relationships, thoughts, and intimacy that make up a life of significance. Attention to a precious moment, when lost, cannot be reclaimed. Withdrawal into a technological screen circumvents the opportunity for personal insight, bonding with others, and nourishing internal wisdom.

Technology is sold as a means to connect and communicate with people. The equipment is simple to purchase and use, but the simplistic and vacuous "connections" that are sold are absent of true feeling and genuine associations. Personal understanding cannot be communicated via text messages, emails, or Facebook postings. Connecting with a human being is much different from simplistic contacts, in which any true understanding of the person is nonexistent.

Messaging "I'm sorry for your loss" when a person's child, parent, spouse, or friend dies falls leaden on the person's soul. Being present and sitting quietly with the person speaks much louder than a text and crying emojis. While the thought may be genuine, how it is expressed does matter. Personal connection matters.

A case can be made today that technology does not bring society together but divides it. Incivility is expressed easily in social media and through technology. Being buried in technology can create remoteness and isolation. The glib phrases and mottoes of technology companies speak glowingly of connections, but in reality, being connected requires an understanding of oneself and others and cannot be created simply by algorithmic calculations. Emotional and heartfelt relationships are not conducive to screens. Energy, closeness, and passion are too human to be communicated by technology. Diversion is contrary to connection and to a path of self-discovery.

Children are lost in their phones while out to dinner with their parents. Young adults on a date are distracted by text and email notifications. Grandparents have to text grandchildren and do not get to hear their voice or emotional inflection. In reality, texts are just electronic telegrams. Young children entertain themselves through games, movies, and websites, which distracts them from being present, in the moment, and interacting with others.

The issue is this: Can a child or adult find a sense of self via technology? Having one's head buried in a screen and seeing nonevents will not uncover or enhance a sense of self and humanity. The screen flickers, and with it, self-understanding and meaning are ignored.

Success is not to be found in video games or virtual experiences. In fact, some computer "games" are devoid of ethical and moral values; winning at all costs is the best course of action. Many of them are geared to violence, where one "wins" if one's death ratio is greater than that of one's opponent. Ethical lessons and values are not even alluded to; simply winning is important. Emotionally empty-headed technological activity does not result in accomplishment.

Being present in reality—the here and now—provides the ability to learn, be creative, look inside oneself, be accountable, and love and sense the humanity of others. Looking outside of oneself opens doors to true human connection and making true friends instead of just racking up statistics on a page of code. Relationships are real, not virtual.

Imagination comes from within and through experiences. Growth of self requires independence from others, at times, but also from technology.

If life is losing its luster, it may be because individuals have made an initial choice to shield themselves from the effort and pain of it and seek redress in the isolation of technology and away from the complexities of relationships and the mirror of self-reflection.

Spiders and Flies

Like spiders
We sit
Caught in the web
Spun by regulation
Trapped in our linear minds
That bark for a life
That doesn't exist.
The black widows
Sting
And paralyze
Through reports
And data,
Bogus measurability
That pretends to
Speak the truth.
Like flies

Bound
In our gossamer chains
Of our own creation
Immobilized by
Our false need for certainty
We strangle the creativity
Of our calling.

WHAT TO REMEMBER

- A person's view of himself or herself might be much different from what others believe that person to be.
- "Being" has to do with the authority and uniqueness of each person based on values, beliefs, and integrity.
- Finding oneself involves accepting the internal changes that may be required to develop a sense of personal "being."
- Growing into maturity involves an understanding of the difference between needs and wants.
- Parental influence is great. The loss of a parent equates to the loss of an anchor and can impose a sense of rootlessness on children.
- Individuals with a high sense of self-esteem have well-articulated views of self. Those with low levels have inconsistent, uncertain, and unstable views of self.
- Technology is sold as a means to connect with others, but it can sidetrack people into personal silos of relationships or thought patterns with others.
- Failure and defeat can create the fabric for "new beginnings" if individuals learn from them.

NOTES

1. Eckhart, Meister, Eckhart Society, https://www.eckhartsociety.org.

2. McLeod, Saul, "Carl Rogers," Simply Psychology, https://www.simplypsychology.org/carl-rogers.html.

3. McLeod, "Carl Rogers."

4. Burns, James MacGregor, *Transforming Leadership* (New York: Atlantic Monthly Press, 2003), 144.

5. Pruett, Kyle, *Me, Myself, and I* (New York: Goddard Press, 1999), 50.

6. Harris, Maxine, *The Loss That Is Forever* (New York: Penguin Books, 1995), 14.

7. Bower, Claire A., "From a Child's Eyes: Loss, Growth and Purpose," *Every Mother Counts*, April 1, 2016, https://blog.everymothercounts.org/from-a-childs-eyes-loss-growth-and-purpose-dc986e157c72.

8. Harris, *Loss That Is Forever*, 109.

9. Harris, *Loss That Is Forever*, 109.

10. Popova, Maria, "Nietzsche on How to Find Yourself and the True Value of Education," Brain Pickings, https://www.brainpickings.org/2015/09/30/nietzsche-find-yourself-schopenhauer-as-educator/.

11. Ibid.

12. Hock, Dee, *Birth of the Choardic Age* (San Francisco: Berrett-Koehler Publishers, 1999), 224.

4

BARNACLES, HIGH WIRES, AND MINDSETS

Life is the art of drawing without any eraser.
—John W. Gardner

Failure is a powerful moat that can separate people from their lives and possibilities. In many cases, fear of failure can dash the hopes and desires individuals have for their lives.

Parents and others have expectations and aspirations for children and young adults that are intended to be helpful and supportive. For some, however, these aims and ambitions create the pressure of failure and letting others down that can cement people in place. As John Gardner stated, "The barnacle is confronted with an existential decision about where it's going to live. Once it decides . . . it spends the rest of its life with its head cemented to a rock."[1]

Like the barnacle, fearing failure and not meeting expectations can cement individuals in place and stop them from pushing ahead with their dreams or goals. They cease learning and growing, can become lethargic and apathetic, and can start to rigidify. Options close and opportunities shrink.

In the United States, citizens applaud success and decry failure. There aren't just stars, there are superstars, megastars, and idols. They are held up to youngsters as models of success; in a few cases, they are cited as possible presidential material, even though they have little or no political or executive experience. But they are famous, and their script and public relations pabulum create an image of intelligence and personality.

Failure brings an entirely different perspective. Synonyms for *failure* include *mistake, blooper, fiasco, loss, blunder, botch,* and *bungle,* among others. As the old saying goes, "Success has many fathers, but failure is an orphan."

Failure can be painful. Not meeting expectations—personal or others—is tough. At times, it is the result of poor performance, wrong strategy, or lack of personal commitment. In any case, the mark was missed, and direction and motivation were lost. Disappointing others can also scar reputation and relationships. Sometimes it can be embarrassing if failed personal or professional judgments and decisions are publicized. Reputation and self-image can be damaged.

The poet David Whyte stated, "The difficult point about any sudden loss of direction, any fear that holds us back from new territory, is that we begin to think that we may be frauds, that everything that led up to this experience may have been manufactured, too."[2] Whyte is accurate in the sense that falling short affects self-concept and confidence— "Maybe I'm not as good as I (or others) think"—and may result in second-guessing oneself—"Am I an all-talk, no-action person?"—and thinking about how not to fail—"I should not have taken the risk"— which can have a contrary effect.

HIGH-WIRE THINKING

Karl Wallenda was a high-wire artist who did very dangerous tightrope walking. Conventional wisdom would assert that he probably placed all his thoughts and plans around how to not fall and to remain safe. However, he thought that fearing failure and being afraid of falling get in the way. The "Wallenda factor" was the "capacity to embrace positive goals, to pour one's energies into the task, not looking behind and dredging up excuses for past events."[3]

Individuals must set positive goals. Dredging up negative issues or fears that occurred in the past stymies progress. Bemoaning the "ghosts of the past" is not productive for the future. Looking ahead and learning from prior experience are positives; however, anxiety, which burns energy and raises self-pity over one's past shortcomings is not helpful in any way. Engaging in this type of self-destructive behavior works against future success.

A major self-concept issue for people in this situation is not failure but whether they picked themselves up and moved ahead. Resilience. What, if anything, did they do to collaborate in their own defeat? Defeats and failures provide the fabric for new beginnings, open self-awareness and perspective, and activate the human spirit. Learning what one does well and what is difficult comes with honest introspection and cognitive analysis.

Self-efficacy—the innate belief that one can achieve goals and deal with prospective situations—influences the effort to persevere in tough and complicated situations. Leaders and others learn from hardships and failure.

Hardships teach individuals to cope with situations beyond their control as well as recognize their limits and blind spots. In these situations, compassion and sensitivity are necessary, along with understanding what really matters. Challenges, successes, and defeats not only open up new points of view but also expose blind spots. No one is free of pain, but that pain can also bring insight and self-discovery.

Solitude is necessary to listen to one's inner voice. Living in the cacophony of social media and technology drowns out the internal muse that whispers insights, creativity, and wisdom. Solitude is not always about the absence of other people, but it certainly means being present and connected to oneself.

Courage is required to withdraw from social networks and groups and instead reflect on and discover what is percolating internally. Being along can light the lamp of desire and uncover the course to greater meaning. This requires looking deeper inside oneself and taking the risk to stand on principles. In doing so, the truth of oneself becomes more apparent and uncovers a sense of meaning and integrity.

SOLITUDE AND STRESS

Solitude, being alone, is something many people fear. But others opt for solitude voluntarily. Solitude provides the ability to self-reflect and find things within oneself that can lead to creativity and new beginnings. Insight comes in these times of self-reflection, moving people in new directions or removing them from endeavors or situations that are contrary to their beliefs

Many artists from all disciplines find respite in solitude. Cognitive reflection is one thing, but understanding one's emotional tenor is also important. Sitting with oneself and letting the mind and heart flow enable awareness and understanding. But preparing for self-reflection can be difficult. Too often our society interrupts or deters the opportunity to find the necessary quiet solitude. Technology and social contexts and expectations get in the way.

Solitude and isolation are not the same: solitude is selected and strictly voluntary; isolation is not. At times, socially or legally, individuals are isolated because of the perception of others or through the justice system and other systems. Social isolation occurs between couples, friends, or groups if there is some manner of conflict or discord. People are shut off socially from interacting with others.

At times, solitude is essential in leadership. While leaders must have connections with people in order to function properly, there are times, particularly in highly difficult situations, where leaders must decide and act on their own reflection, analysis, and values to move ahead with moral virtue. In these difficult times, there may be a number of options and variables to consider that are controversial and not universally accepted. Leaders, however, must act on their own interpretations and consider what is best even though some will not agree. To do so requires introspection and contemplation.

Stress is evident in life, and different people feel and respond to it differently. Solitude and reflection can help individuals untangle knots of stress and fears and find a course that adheres to values and commitments. Complicated and perplexing issues are generally stressful because of the outcomes that are at stake. Stress is inevitable at times, but it doesn't have to be debilitating and is often the forerunner to confronting great opportunities.

Children feel stress too. Trying to achieve in school or other venues is stressful. Children feel pressure to conform to group norms and others' expectations and to be accepted. Adults and others face self-doubts about their competence and abilities in the face of work or turmoil. Health issues bring stress; personal relationships and certainly environmental and financial issues can be draining. Adolescents and adults of all ages frequently refer to themselves as "stressed out."

Life can be hectic, and uncertainties can be traumatic. Society, workplace, and family demands together with personal perspectives can produce a stressful stew. Time and solitude become difficult to plan and control. Social, corporate, or family cultures can be very demanding and not always considerate of the needs of the individual. People frequently take on new roles or jobs that carry with them different expectations, which also generates some stress.

Time pressure is a stressor: things have to get accomplished in a timely manner or there will be major consequences. Frequently, decisions must be made immediately or within a short time frame. Not having adequate time to make thorough judgments turns the clock into an important factor. History demonstrates that time is not always available to make critical decisions.

"Having it all" in today's society puts people in positions of expecting and doing too much, some of which may not be rewarding or fulfilling. Money is a real stressor. In some cases, the loss of a job and fiscal independence can dash hopes and dreams. Severe economic issues can cost individuals their general independence and the opportunity to find personal satisfaction. Loneliness—which is different from solitude— affects lifespan and health. In negative circumstances, people begin to see life differently and adopt a mindset that is less than optimistic.

MINDSETS

How people perceive themselves has a major effect on how they live their lives. Their belief systems are powerful predictors of their success. What they believe about their potential and their abilities influence their standpoint and behavior when confronting challenges.

A person's self-image influences whether the person will become whoever he or she may want to be and whether the person can achieve the things he or she values. Personal beliefs, conscious and unconscious, and self-perception eventually translate into decisions and actions—affecting relationships, achievement, resilience, and learning.

Carol Dweck, in her book *Mindset*, discusses the impact of the mindset people adopt. She indicates that there are two basic mindsets: fixed and growth. Dweck asserts that some individuals believe their qualities are fixed—carved in stone. These individuals believe their intelligence is fixed and their personality and moral character are established.

They further believe that creativity, character, and intelligence can't be changed or improved significantly, which means success is proof of inherent ability and intelligence. This creates the urgency to prove themselves over and over again. Consequently, avoiding failure at all costs verifies their intelligence and ability. "Every situation calls for a confirmation of their intelligence, personality, or character. Every situation is evaluated: Will I succeed or fail? Will I look smart or dumb? Will I be accepted or rejected? Will I feel like a winner or a loser?"[4]

Individuals with a fixed mindset opt for success over growth to prove they are special—different from and better than other people. Specialness is distinct from uniqueness. Everyone is a unique, one-of-a-kind person. Those who consider themselves special feel that they are better than others—more important, more valuable. And when things go wrong, they lose focus and blame others.

Dweck indicates that the self-esteem movement encourages specialness as superiority. She says that this movement has helped individuals confirm their superiority. "My favorite was the 'I Love Me mirror,' a mirror with I Love Me in huge capital letters written across the bottom half. By looking into it, you can administer the message to yourself and not wait for the outside world to announce your specialness."[5]

A growth mindset, on the other hand, has a very different perspective, "based on the belief that your basic qualities are things you can cultivate through your efforts . . . everyone can change and grow through application and experience."[6] People with a growth mindset believe their basic qualities are open and can be refined and enhanced. Hard work and perseverance enhance performance. Talent, temperament, and ability change and grow with effort. The door to the future is open, not closed, to greater development and maturation.

Contrary to those with a fixed mindset, individuals with a growth mindset believe that a person's potential is unknown and that through toil, passion, and training, things get accomplished as they grow. Failure is not a disaster but is an opportunity for learning and stretching skills and outlooks.

Ability is not static or cemented in permanence. People differ in talents and skills, aptitudes and interest, but those with a growth mindset believe that issues can be confronted, understood, and addressed, and learning can take place.

People with a growth mindset challenge themselves and recognize the value of effort. Challenges are not seen as possible indictments of one's intelligence or skill. Instead, the love of facing challenges, applying effort, and being resilient creates insight and learning. Fear of failure, as indicated earlier, imprisons people in a cell of stagnation; people with a growth mindset see challenges and do not succumb to fear.

As with many things, individuals have a choice. Because mindsets are beliefs, each person has a choice as to what mindset to adopt and assume. As the eminent sociologist Benjamin Barber stated, "I don't divide the world into the weak and the strong, or the successes and the failures. . . . I divide the world into the learners and non-learners."[7]

Disequilibrium

Equilibrium lives!
that's what some think
as change moves the ground
beneath their quaking feet.
Chaos, they feel, shines
the light of weakness on them.
Not to be in control is
a rebuke of their ability,
and shows to the world
weakness and fecklessness.
But shunning disequilibrium
is rebuking life itself
as change is constant and
transitions are the staple of life.

WHAT TO REMEMBER

- Fearing failure is destabilizing and can cement individuals in place, unable to move forward.
- Stress can have a devastating effect on an individual's roles and happiness.
- Positive thinking and goals can uplift individuals to successfully confront difficult issues.

- People learn from hardships and failure, and solitude opens the doors to insight and wisdom.
- Individuals determine whether they adopt a fixed or growth mindset.

NOTES

1. Gardner, John, *Living, Leading, and the American Dream* (San Francisco: Jossey-Bass, 2003), 41.

2. Whyte, David, *Crossing the Unknown Sea* (New York: Riverhead Books, 2001), 155.

3. Bennis, Warren, and Burt Nanus, *Leaders: The Strategies for Taking Charge* (New York: Harper and Row, 1985), 71.

4. Dweck, Carol S. *Mindset* (New York: Ballantine Books, 2008), 6.

5. Dweck, *Mindset*, 30.

6. Dweck, *Mindset*, 7.

7. Dweck, *Mindset*, 16.

5

ME, MYSELF, AND I

To be nobody-but-yourself—in a world which is doing its best, night and day, to make you everybody else—means to fight the hardest battle which any human being can fight.

—e. e. cummings

At bottom every human being understands very well that he is entirely unique on this earth and then not even the strangest coincidence will ever again throw together such curiously multifarious ingredients into the single thing that he is; he knows, yet he hides it like a guilty conscience—but why? Because he fears his neighbor, who demands conventional behavior and disguises himself with it.

—Friedrich Nietzsche

Looking in the mirror isn't always easy. The young face of the past slowly evolves, replaced by one lined with sentiment, ventures, and time. The passage of time sparks thoughts and memories of the past. An expression raises recollections of Mom or Dad. The eyes sparkle green just like Grandma's. The scar on the side of the chin flashes memories of a hockey game at the age of fourteen. To others, there are no stories in that impression in the mirror, just distinctive physical traits and expressions. The mirror communicates body image but falls short of the mental image people have of themselves.

As Pam Morris puts it, "Only I know and see the face in the mirror as I generally am. The reflection in my mirror is the effect of all my life's experiences that only I can present. Given that I have the final say how to represent myself in a world that is repeatedly changing it is vital how I interact with the reflection in my mirror."[1]

Physical appearance is one thing, but the "self" is another. Body and self are not synonymous. The mind, ego, spirit, and self form the real essence of a person but are invisible to the eye. Questions exist in every person about the self—who the person really is.

The circumstances of a person's upbringing are quite influential, as the perspectives and attitudes of the various generations demonstrate. For example, baby boomers view life differently from millennials. Older generations have a deeper point of view and are experienced in facing life and everything it brings. The viewpoint of today's youth comes without the experience of confronting the diverse complexities and vagaries of life over an extended time. Idealism lives within the hearts of youth, and pragmatism lies in wait in experienced minds.

Life is a continual process of discovery. People continue to uncover who they are as they move through life. The self is not static, not frozen in time. Individuals reinvent themselves through experience and self-reflection as they confront challenges to their integrity, to their principles and values. An obvious prerequisite is defining the standards by which one lives, because they are the foundation for reflection and decisions.

Discomfort is not unusual. Youthful introspection brings change as people discover and assess who they want to be versus who they perceive they are. Self-reflection is an ongoing process; individuals rethink and reframe their sense of identity as they compare reality to their beliefs, ambitions, and dreams.

Social, cultural, economic, and historical contexts provide the foundation for identity. Erik Erikson stated, "We deal with a process 'located' *in the core of the individual* and yet also *in the core of his communal culture*, a process which establishes, in fact, the identity of those two identities. . . . In psychological terms, identity formation employs a process of simultaneous reflection and observation, a process taking place on all levels of mental functioning, by which the individual judges himself in light of what he perceives to be the way in which others judge him in comparison to themselves and to a typology significant to them."[2]

SELF-IDENTITY

Self basically comprises the perceptions and beliefs individuals have about themselves. However, their view may not be congruent with how others perceive them. A sense of self-worth—what people think of themselves in terms of their values, abilities, and potential—is important. Self-image has two aspects: body image and external personality. Almost everyone has a need to be regarded positively or, at least, respectfully by others.

In adolescent years, with brain growth and the development of abstract thought, individuals interact in more complex ways. They begin to perceive themselves differently and begin to ask themselves questions like:

- What am I good at?
- How do others perceive me?
- What kind of person am I?
- What will I do in the future?

Aspects of adolescent egocentrism affect how they view themselves. According to Rosemary Barnett,[3] there are a few images to consider:

- Imaginary Audience. Teens think of themselves as always being onstage, with everyone watching them, paying attention to what they do, and listening to everything they say. They are very sensitive about criticism at this point.
- Personal Fable. By thinking everyone is looking at them, they get an inflated opinion of themselves and their own importance. During this phase, they believe they definitely will reach great heights of accomplishment—become famous and rich, become a professional athlete or actor. They feel invincible.
- Optimistic Bias. In this third perspective, they may take risks at times—driving a car, engaging in intimate relationships, and indulging in unpredictable and impulsive activities. They believe they are going to be great, and if someone raises a negative, they respond, "It can't happen to me."

As adolescents mature in their ability to think abstractly, these three thought patterns about themselves eventually diminish; childhood imaginings succumb to reality, which is not always an easy transition. Dreams and ambitions may fade, but points of view and desires blossom. As things unfold, adolescents confront the realities of their successes as well as their limitations.

Erikson indicated that in adolescence, youth must confront life "crises."[4] The first crisis, which occurs in middle adolescence, is the "crisis of identity versus identity confusion." The issue is finding balance between developing a unique self-identity while still "fitting in" with the group—a struggle between determining who teens want to be and how others regard them. Do they push ahead with their own perspective or succumb to the views of others?

Traversing this crisis successfully results in a clear picture of the individual's identity that the individual can share with others. In order to become an emotionally mature adult, one must be confident and clear about who one is. Trying to be another person eventually creates an issue of inauthenticity and personal distress and fear.

Being accepted for "who you are" is a gift, and it is necessary for social or intimate relationships. Acceptance of self and others is basic in order to be able to reveal one's true self. Conforming to other's attitudes, philosophies, or perspectives can destroy one's sense of independence and eventually spirit and integrity.

In late adolescence, the second crisis concerns intimacy versus isolation, which represents the struggle to achieve a mutual balance between giving love and support and receiving them. Adolescents must figure out how to initiate and maintain close friends outside of family and eventually move to have reciprocal romantic relationships in early adulthood. The result is development of the ability to maintain modest and mutual relationships and to bond with others to achieve common goals. Those who do not develop this ability can become distant and self-contained or, conversely, dependent, needy, and vulnerable.

Adults construct and reconstruct their identity. Interactions, experiences, introspection, and self-reflection mitigate change. In relationships, conscious and unconscious understandings occur and open the door to developing a unique sense of self along with greater empathy and understanding. Creating a sense of self-definition may depart from family norms and expectations and result in greater independence.

Changes in each stage of life and moving to the unknown can create a sense of ending and fear for a new or different beginning. Jacques

Barzun wrote, "But when the will to self-searching has you by the throat, there is immense value in being able to find a Self: that is to say, a solid entity that you can trust, because you made it yourself and made it well. A well-made Self is not a haphazard collection of habits and prejudices, of notions and fancies; it is an ordered set of reflections, conclusions, and convictions."[5]

SELF AND RELATIONSHIPS

Relationships with others offer major opportunities to learn important lessons and discover "who we are, what we fear, where our power comes from, and the meaning of true love."[6] Not all relationships are happy. Some are challenging, annoying, frustrating, and emotionally heartbreaking. Others are difficult because individuals themselves are negative and fail to recognize their own dark side and cynicism. Success happens, but so do setbacks, and individuals get a view of themselves in, and learn from, both types of situations.

Elisabeth Kubler-Ross stated, "We often look to others to define us. If others are in a bad mood, we are brought down. If others see us as being wrong, we become defensive. But who we are is beyond attack and defense. We are whole, complete, and of worth just as we are, whether we are rich or poor, old or young, receiving an Olympic gold medal, or beginning or ending a relationship. Whether at the beginning or end of life, at the height of fame or the depths of despair, we are always the people behind our circumstances."[7]

Standing for principle and beliefs reinforces one's sense of self. Being at peace in body, mind, and spirit provides inner integrity. Doing things to win the approval of others is futile and indicates a loss of self-worth. If individuals are perceived positively, they are not treated negatively or as "bad" persons. They are loved and accepted for who they are, unconditionally. People of all ages need to be considered positively and valued by others for who they are.

Respect and acceptance are those relational qualities everyone seeks. However, that does not mean that people have to conform or be compliant to others' expectations. Individuals can be respected even if their views are different; being uncivil to a person for his or her opinions is not a model of respect.

Civility does not mean agreement but does require deference to principles of character and courtesy. Politeness and mutual respect are evident.

Conditional love results in one's acting not on the basis of who one is but on getting the approval of others. Some children feel that if they don't do what others desire, they will not be loved, a belief that can live with them the rest of their lives and cause them much difficulty. Conditional love is not loving the individual as a distinctive being. In essence, it requires the "loved one" to meet the other's expectation and requirements. Behaving as the person another individual desires is not a course to self-fulfillment.

Giving unconditional love means letting individuals be uniquely themselves with their talents, skills, and perspectives. No conditions or limitations are evident when someone is loved unconditionally. A person's true self can shine. Unconditional love is selfless: it does not require anything back and never asks, "What's in it for me?"

The closer individuals meet their self-image, the higher their sense of self-worth, which is important in achieving self-actualization. This ideal self is dynamic and changes with goals and ambitions.

A SELF-MADE IDENTITY

John O'Donohue stated, "There are no manuals for the construction of the individual you would like to become. You are the only one who can decide this and take up the lifetime of work that it demands. This is such a wonderful privilege and such an exciting adventure. To grow into the person that your deepest longing desires is a great blessing. If you can find a creative harmony between your soul and your life, you'll have found something infinitely precious."[8]

A sense of being doesn't come easily. Growing into maturity requires a lot of internal work. People's developmental process includes who they were, who they are, and who they will become. Pressure about identity is often related to external roles and positions rather than internal desires and aspirations. Self-concept can be structured around gender, ethnicity, race, age, or even academic standing. Some perceive themselves in an individualistic way as a "me" self; others see themselves collectively as an "us" self.

Self-concept is a powerful force influencing an individual's thoughts, feelings, and behavior. In a way, it helps individuals make sense of things and understand their emotions and impact on daily interactions and life. With a sense of self-efficacy, individuals have a sense about their ability to apply their skills and abilities: how well they can mobilize resources, determine behavior, and make decisions to accomplish goals.

Self-understanding includes the convictions and beliefs that provide the stimulus and discipline to move ahead. Barzun believes that individuals should "cultivate their gardens" by attending to what they are fit to do. In this view, individuals are both "being" and "becoming." Life has continuous changes and new beginnings; it is not static, premade, or a replica.

Values, ethics, and principles are the basis for action with integrity that reflects the true self. Being true to oneself is not always easy, because life plays out with difficult and intimidating forces that are outside an individual's control and difficult to confront. Satisfaction and happiness in life come from living in harmony with standards and values and the rules one creates for oneself in pursuit of ambitions. A broader sense of self involves values, beliefs, and principles that move beyond ego.

SELF AND EGO

"While the self brought the gift of personal freedom, it also spun another veil . . . : the illusions of the ego."[9] Mihaly Csikszentmihalyi stated that selfishness has been and will be a part of living. The ego uses possessions as an indication of the owner's power, standing, and competence. According to this standard, the more one has, the greater one is. Some individuals connect self-esteem to material things and specific relationships. Objects provide concrete evidence of influence and power as seen in society's preoccupation with materialism.

Frequently, ego is centered on competition and comparisons of others. Being recognized and part of the "in" group is important. The fear of being left out or not recognized is pervasive. Craving recognition is important to adolescents, and frequently, the means to obtain it emanates from their collection of objects and material goods. Recognition for intellectual or creative ability is difficult because neither is always tangible at this age.

Individuals sometimes use relationships with others to build their own image and serve their ego. Such behavior reflects a lack of care for the well-being of those others, as long as the individuals get the personal effect they desire. Pervasive among members of society are comparisons to others and their lifestyle and achievements, along with feelings of jealousy when others succeed or do well. Some feel that another person's achievements and recognition deny their own abilities and accomplishments.

Ego also blames others when things go wrong or problems occur. Failure cannot be accepted, and losing is not good for ego-driven reputations. The ego finds others to condemn, and as such, relationships and respect wither.

Within each person is an inner voice no one else can hear. According to Singer, it is the mental dialog that goes on inside an individual's head. In a sense, it is "you who's talking and it's you who is listening."[10] Opportunities or failures, prospects and outcomes, swirl in the mind.

Frequently, this inner voice raises questions and issues about the possibilities and circumstances being confronted. Frequently, the inner voice also raises matters of ethics and beliefs and right and wrong and desires and expectations. At times, the voice will bark, and other times it is subtle. Individuals have to determine whether or not to listen, because sometimes the voice raises uncomfortable issues that individuals want to ignore and not think about.

New or changing circumstances can raise consternation because they may bring about challenges, the depth of which may not be known or understood. As people mature, they become more aware of their abilities and a sense of what they can offer, hopefully learning from failures and hardships.

Self-reflective people develop the ability to cope with issues beyond their control because they recognize limits and blind spots and are clear about what matters in life. They have the sensitivity and flexibility needed to traverse those times. Understanding self, being aware of one's strengths and weaknesses, supports the ability to respond to circumstances with integrity. Without self-understanding, individuals live an unstable life influenced by social, business, or relationship pressures.

Self-knowledge brings certain advantages: better decision-making, less inner conflict, greater self-control, resistance to social pressure, and tolerance and understanding of others. Being true to oneself is a strong foundation for living life and finding meaning and happiness.

According to Carl Rogers, there are five characteristics of fully functioning people:[11]

- They are open to experience, both positive and negative, and confront both and work through them.
- They trust feelings, recognize their feelings and intuitions, and address them to make appropriate decisions.
- They seek creativity and take risks to try new things to expand their life. They adjust to new circumstances and change.
- They seek existential living and are present and able to appreciate life's moments and avoid prejudice and preconceptions.
- They live a fulfilling life and look for new experiences and challenges to find satisfaction in life.

People have a desire to self-actualize and work to fulfill their potential and aspirations. They understand themselves—the potential within themselves—seek experiences to fulfill themselves, and recognize their obligations and commitments.

Self and I

The self, the I, the me
Are never all there for you to see
They hide as reluctant friends
In dark shadows with curious ends
I urge them to wander out
Usually in times of serious doubt.
The self, the I, the me
Hold true virtue and the key
To who inhabits the depths of my soul
And who suffers when I am not whole
So celebrate the self, the I, the me
And light them up for all to see.

WHAT TO REMEMBER

- Relationships present opportunities to learn about and discover one-self.
- Adolescents' egocentrism affects how they think of themselves. They feel they have an audience, examine how others see them, develop a personal fable, and create an optimistic bias, which includes the concept of invincibility.
- Adolescents question what they are good at and how they are perceived; and they examine the kind of person they are and what the future holds.
- Unconditional love accepts individuals as they are, whereas conditional love is based on individuals conforming to desired qualities or conditions.
- Congruence between self-image and self-worth is important in achieving self-actualization.
- Ego frequently is centered on comparisons and competition and on the acquisition of material goods and wealth.
- An inner voice exists within people that raises perspectives and questions about issues and possibilities.
- Self-understanding creates better decisions, self-control, tolerance, and understanding.

NOTES

1. Morris, Pam, "Inside Every Person You Know, There Is a Person You Don't Know: The Reflection in the Mirror," https://letterpile.com/inspirational/httphubpagescomhub-The-Reflection-in-my-Mirror.

2. Erikson, Erik H., *Identity: Youth and Crisis* (New York: W. W. Norton & Company, 1968), 22.

3. Barnett, Rosemary V., "Helping Teens Answer the Question 'Who Am I?': Cognitive Development in Adolescence." ResearchGate, 2019, https://www.researchgate.net/publication/239531192_Helping_Teens_Answer_the_Question_Who_Am_I_Cognitive_Development_in_Adolescents.

4. Erikson, *Identity*, 131–36.

5. Barzun, Jacques, *Begin Here* (Chicago: University of Chicago Press, 1991), 199.

6. Kubler-Ross, Elisabeth, and David Kessler, *Life Lessons* (New York: Scribner, 2000), 60.

7. Kubler-Ross, *Begin Here*, 32.

8. O'Donohue, John, *Eternal Echoes* (New York: HarperCollins, 1999), 102.

9. Csikszentmihalyi, Mihaly, *The Evolving Self* (New York: HarperPerennial, 1993), 77.

10. Singer, Michael A., *The Untethered Soul: The Journey beyond Yourself* (New Harbinger Publications, 2007), 8, Kindle.

11. McLeod, Saul, "Carl Rogers," Simply Psychology, https://www.simplypsychology.org/carl-rogers.html.

6

MEANING OR DECADENCE?

Character—the willingness to accept responsibility for one's own life—is the source from which self-respect springs.

—Joan Didion

In the last analysis the individual is responsible for living his own life "finding himself." If he persists in shifting the responsibility to someone else, he fails to find out the meaning of his own existence.

—Thomas Merton

Life can seem confusing, like assembling one thousand pieces of an abstract puzzle without a clear picture of the final image. Lives emerge and are pieced together by inclinations, decisions, intuition, emotions, and relationships, hopefully predicated on clear and honorable values and principles.

Everyone, eventually, faces the question, Why am I here? Children do not think about it much. Doing what they are told, meeting parents' expectations, following school rules and family rituals go on generally without question. Being a son, daughter, or student comes with prescribed expectations and behavior. Thinking beyond into a more philosophical or futuristic realm is beyond a child's developmental level.

For adolescents, things begin to change a bit. People ask them about their dreams and future aspirations. Many focus on their physical skills and their contemporary heroes. Playing hockey for the Chicago Blackhawks, being a lead singer in a rock band, or having the lead in Hollywood movies are not unusual aspirations. Of course, all of these successes come with recognition and materialistic goods: cars, cash, and condos.

The vision changes with high school graduation and the dramatic change lurking on the horizon. All of a sudden, many parental and educational mandates evaporate, and the latitude for individual decisions and responsibility widens. As Robert Redford stated as the character Bill McKay, the longshot election winner in the movie *The Candidate*, "What do we do now?" Many young adults think this is when the blank canvas of life stares back at them. Certainly, travel, college, and jobs come to mind. A new era of greater autonomy and individual choice opens to them. But where to start? Where to go? Can I do it?

At this stage, students have some idea of their strengths, skills, and interests, all of which cause them to gravitate to certain areas or careers. But even these perspectives are speculative as they face and grasp situations and gain greater understanding of internal and external realities and demands. "What do I want my life to be?" rings in their ears now and probably consistently in the future. Their approach and choices are made as the responsibility of adulthood gains momentum.

What they do not realize is that the question "Who am I?" involves learning from errors mistakes, accountability, and limits. As Parker Palmer stated, "I have no idea how I could have learned the truth about myself without the mistakes I have made."[1] Stepping off into a new phase of life raises some inevitable issues.

Pragmatism seems to rule: the bottom tier of Maslow's hierarchy of basic security and fiscal needs takes priority. "I have to make money." "I need a place to live." "I have to take care of myself." "Self-actualization" is not directly on new high school graduates' radar in these conversations, because many individuals feel that everything will take care of itself if economic security is at hand and the doors to greater independence and relationships open.

Philosophy and finding purpose often clash with pragmatism. The question is raised when a student says, "I really want to be a writer—a journalist maybe. But my mom wants me to be a lawyer. She says there are hundreds of unemployed writers and actors serving tea and crumpets in New York. The arts are fine for a hobby, but not for earning a living." The mother's views raise questions about making a living versus living life. Are they mutually exclusive? Or do both paths provide the knowledge and wisdom for finding a life of meaning that is in harmony with interests and talents?

GENERATIONS AND CONTEXT

The context in which a person lives, influences and shapes the person's self-identity. Context includes parents, schooling, and the greater social, political, and economic culture. Sometimes individuals get others to endorse their identity or they change their own behavior to comply with others' expectations. The individualistic self "focuses on how one is separate and different from others."[2]

Each generation faces a different social context from the previous one. History's impact, through economic depressions, booming economies, world wars, technological advances, and other changes in social norms, creates distinct attitudes and viewpoints that dwell in people's minds and memories throughout their lives. Perspectives and priorities are formulated in part because of the context in which they were raised.

The impact of social institutions—religion, education, politics, law, media, and others—affects the individual's point of view and mindset. Whether one was raised during the Great Depression or the Vietnam War influences perceptions of life and priorities differently from those who were born in 2000. Generational perspectives, consequently, can differ with regard to relationships and priorities as well as roles in a diverse society. These changes raise conflict over expectations and responsibility.

The generation in which people were born certainly involves the impact of the events and issues at that time. All members of an age group are repositories of the history of the period in which they were raised. Baby boomers have a different perspective than millennials on some things. Each generation experiences transitions. Today, the most obvious one is a transition from the industrial to the technological age, complete with its impact on education, employment, communication, entertainment, and family life.

A study by the Pew Research Center illustrates the difference between millennials (ages twenty-three to thirty-eight in 2019) and the silent generation (ages seventy-four to ninety-one in 2019), basically comparing today's young adults to their grandparents. The report states the past five decades "have seen large shifts in U.S society and culture. It has been a period in which Americans, especially Millennials, have become more detached from major institutions such as political parties, religion, the military and marriage. At the same time, the racial and ethnic make-up of the country has changed, college attainment has spiked and women have greatly increased their participation in the nation's workforce."[3]

The study also determined that:

- Today's young adults are better educated than members of the silent generation are.
- A greater share of millennial women have bachelor's degrees than their male counterparts, which is a reversal from the silent generation.
- Women today are more likely to be working in their adult years than women in the past were.
- Millennials are three times as likely to have never married when they were young as those in the silent generation.
- Men in the silent generation are ten times more likely to be veterans than those in the millennial generation are.
- Greater numbers of millennials lived in metropolitan areas from a young age than did members of the silent generation.

Another Pew Research Center study tracked the opinions of the different generations on politics and other issues.[4] They found that with regard to political parties, 59 percent of millennials are Democrats. Among Gen Xers and boomers, 48 percent describe themselves as Democrats. However, a majority of the silent generation (52 percent) indicates a Republican preference.

Regarding the political issue of the size and scope of government, 51 percent and 50 percent of the millennials and Gen Xers, respectively, prefer "bigger government." Boomers and the silent generation prefer smaller government, 57 percent and 70 percent, respectively. On the social issue of same-sex marriage, a majority of the millennials (73 percent), Gen Xers (65 percent), and boomers (56 percent) favor same-sex marriage. Among the silent generation, 44 percent are in favor of same-sex marriage.

Over the last seventy-five years, the role of religion, the structure of families, the economic and employment situations, the impact of technology, and increased access to information and diversion have been transforming influences. Changing norms, social change, parental perspectives, and modifications in values have consequences for the direction of society. In addition, the focus on values and principles comes from wider and more diverse sources. These changes, with their accompanying, dramatic historical events, certainly can alter values and attitudes. Depressions and wars provide extraordinarily different contexts for developing attitudes toward finance and service as well as for careers and education. The social contexts in which people live carry a large influence.

DECAY OR RENEWAL?

Decadence is a strong word, one that is seldom heard today. If it is used, it generally refers to societies and governments of the past. But *decadence* refers to indulgence, decline, moral decay, corruption, and lack of principles, restraints, and self-control. The antonyms for *decadence* include *development, improvement, decency*, as well as *honor, goodness, morality*, and *humility*. The antonyms really describe the qualities most parents desire for their children.

Society today has taken some turns that exemplify a slide into a more decadent path. It is hard to believe that life expectancy in the United States has dropped three years in a row. In the 1960s, the United States had the highest life expectancies in the world. Across the globe, meanwhile, life expectancy is moving upward. The United States is experiencing the longest sustained decline in life expectancy since 1915 to 1918, when the 1918 influenza and World War I were major contributing factors.[5]

Major problems causing the decline in life expectancy are drug overdoses and suicides. Increased deaths among individuals ages twenty-four to forty-four had "an outsized effect" on the statistics, even though baby boomers are aging. Access to synthetic opioids such as fentanyl is growing and is a significant reason for drug abuse issues.

A sense of disconnectedness and hopelessness were identified as reasons for increased drug use, overdoses, and suicides. "Deaths of despair" is a term coined by Ann Case of Princeton University to describe these deaths. Suicides are higher in rural than urban areas.

Today's social context and its influence also raise concerns about individuals' sense of self: who they are and who they may become. In a historical study of empires, Sir John Glubb[6] defined the stages between the rise and the fall of great nations. He cited the following stages: the age of binaries, the age of conquests, the age of commerce, the age of affluence, the age of intellect, and the age of decadence.

Glubb indicated that decadence is characterized by defensiveness, materialism, pessimism, frivolity, weakening of religion, and a welfare state. He also specifies the cause as selfishness, a lost sense of duty, and an extended period of wealth and power. Today's society and culture with their materialistic and narcissistic trends carry some of these qualities.

Jacques Barzun, in a discussion of his book *From Dawn to Decadence*, declared that "decadence means 'falling away, falling apart,' and it happens over and over again in history."[7] The decadence he speaks of may happen in a segment of culture or "pretty much the whole of a culture any given time. . . . People look for something to believe in, and not only believe in the religious sense but believe in the institutional sense."[8]

Barzun indicated that the falling apart of institutions leads to a sense of decadence. Public school failure, government deadlock, separation of the population into ethnic, racial, or other groups, and the abandonment of ethical and moral codes and self-restraint are examples. In addition, he cites the failure of "will" to act and make things better beyond empty slogans.[9]

Margaret Wheatley applied the concept of decadence to today. She stated, "Wealth and power have led to petty and negative behaviors, including narcissism, consumerism, materialism, nihilism, fanaticism, and high levels of frivolity. A celebrity culture worships athletes, actors, and singers. The masses are distracted by entertainment and sporting events, abandon moral restraint, shirk duties, and insist on entitlements. The leaders believe they are impervious and will govern forever."[10]

Wheatley is concerned that a culture focused on the individual leads to polarization, conceit, estrangement, and ultimately loneliness. People emphasize self-interest, not the common good. Popularity is a measure of success: gaining a following, increasing one's number of "friends" per

Facebook's vacuous definition, taking "selfies," and gathering with others in uni-thought silos. Today, people spend time on the internet and other diversionary sources. In addition, a culture of violence is evident in media; this culture is characterized in part by people's verbal assaults on, and desensitization toward, others.

Wheatley states, "The importance of identity as an organizing dynamic for people and all living beings cannot be over emphasized. It always has and forever will be the basis for how we define ourselves as individuals and societies, the choices we make, the things we attend to, the behaviors we manifest."[11]

Every circumstance provides opportunity and possibility for growth or decay. Those with a negative perspective can become complacent, can halt learning, and can imprison themselves in habits through which they seek only comfort and ease. Life becomes stale when that happens; the essence of self-destructive behavior becomes established through self-pity and a victim mentality. Self-imprisonment by one's own attitudes and perspectives is difficult to escape, in part because a person with a negative self-image and a lack of personal accountability paints a dark picture.

People who put themselves on the shelf begin to decay and lose the positive aspirations and attitudes of an earlier life. Frequently, this results in destructive behavior through drugs, alcohol, antagonism, isolation, or anger, all of which can lead to intellectual, social, and physical stagnation and suicide.

New perspectives do not have the soil in which to blossom. Individuals' attitudes and opinions become rigid, and they stop acquiring knowledge and skills. What others think or what they might think or say becomes their focus. They fear other individuals' opinions or perceptions. They become self-victimized by allowing their concern with what others think to constantly resound in their mind.

John Gardner stated, "Creative individuals have the capacity to free themselves from the web of social pressures in which the rest of us are caught. They don't spend time asking 'What will people say?' The fact that 'everybody's doing it' doesn't mean they're doing it. They question assumptions that the rest of us accept."[12] They see what could be and move beyond what people say or believe.

With decay comes conformity. Every society tends toward some kind of conformism. Peer and work groups as well as social media generate conformity in dress, attitude, and behavior. In our modern, complex society, conformity often takes forms that can threaten individuality. Self-renewal, however, requires innovation and change that bring individuals and society as a whole into line with directed purpose and meaning.

A society focused on conformism and the numbing of self-interest and narcissism is headed for the graveyard. The same is true for individuals. In order to meet standards—personal and national—freedom and dignity and a significant measure of independence are required. Seeing beyond pleasure or escape is essential for learning and growth. Maturity requires commitment and recognizes sacrifice, at times, to successfully address life's challenges

Thomas Moore wrote that people express complaints of emptiness, meaninglessness, disillusionment, and depression. These feelings often result in obsessions, addictions, violence, and loss of meaning. The reason, he expressed, was the loss of the "soul." He stated, "Soul is not a thing, but a quality or a dimension of experiencing life and ourselves. It has to do with depth, value, relatedness, part and personal substance."[13] Decadence strips the body as well as the soul and spirit through self-destructive behavior.

A commitment to values moves people toward consistent renewal, not deterioration or complacency. The conformity of silos or groups suffocates the individual who wants to unfold into an independent self. There is a need, when values and standards are on the line, to stand alone—to stand as an autonomous individual, free from anything that scorches one's creative spirit and sense of goodness.

Social media is a powerful force in directing people's attention and, in the process, communicating values. Incivility, fake news, and self-absorption constrain the creation of a sense of community, compassion, and connection. Celebrity culture and its values are detriments to developing a sense of self that incorporates larger ideas and a sense of values and ethics. Narcissism and individualism are not synonymous.

In this milieu, individuals must seriously consider their identity and journey. The allure of materialism and self-centeredness are prominent in many sectors of society; it can be enticing to individuals who are uncertain about who they are and what they want out of life. Chasing a shadow is tiring and never-ending.

As Wheatley says, "Know thyself. What may be less clear . . . is the reason we learn to know ourselves: we develop a knowledge of self so we can give up the self and serve others."[14] Understanding one's self also involves and opens horizons and an appreciation for others and the context in which individuals exist.

Self-identity influences what people are motivated to do and what they think. Desiring to be a part of a peer group—to be popular and to be accepted—comes with hazards. The center focus becomes the group and its norms for acceptance. Hence, in some cases, individuals become involved with drugs or other substances or activities that actually take them out of themselves, out of character, and out of the capacity for rational perception in determining the direction of their lives. Unfortunately, families from all socioeconomic strata have faced this.

In these cases, individuals adapt a "collectivist" self as part of an identified group. Some individuals act in ways that comply with the group—the collective—even if it does not comply with personal perspectives. Being accepted is the goal; the ability to stand apart from the group, which would be an expression of individualism, is not sought. Losing self-identity and self-worth in exchange for group identity is a path to becoming a "lost soul."

While belonging to a group meets some need for acceptance, individuals can lose themselves, their identity, and their uniqueness in order to belong. Individualism has always been an important value in the United States—a cornerstone in art, innovation, and problem solving in a democracy. Autocratic regimes simply require collectivism in behavior and thought.

George Carlin, the noted philosophical comedian, stated that "the larger the group, the more toxic, the more of your beauty as an individual you have to surrender for the sake of group thought. And when you suspend your individual beauty you also give up a lot of your humanity. You do things in the name of a group that you would never do on your own. Injuring, hurting, killing, drinking are all part of it, because you've lost your identity, because you now owe all your allegiance to this thing that's bigger than you are and that controls you."[15] Joy and happiness do not come out of drugs and alcohol or from behavior that is hostile to one's principles and values.

Erich Fromm, in his book *To Have or to Be*, stated, "If I am who I am and not what I have, nobody can deprive me of or threaten my security and my sense of identity. My center is within myself; my capacity for being and for expressing my essential powers is part of my character structure and depends on me."[16]

WHAT WE WISH FOR

People facing frustrating and depressing struggles sometimes spout, "I just want to be happy!" The national motto proclaims one's rights to "life, liberty, and the pursuit of happiness." Pursuing happiness does not necessarily guarantee its attainment: everyone is free to pursue a life that brings happiness and joy—and hopefully fulfillment.

The assumption is that given the liberty to pursue happiness, people would live a good life. Happiness and the good life are frequently used synonymously. But are they the same? The phrase *pursuit of happiness* assumes that happiness is something tangible. But theologian Dietrich Bonhoeffer stated, "What is happiness and unhappiness? It depends so little on the circumstances; it depends really only on that which happens inside a person."[17]

Aristotle indicates that happiness is not about amusement: "Happiness does not lie in amusement; it would, indeed, be strange if the end were amusement, and one were to take trouble and suffer hardship all one's life in order to amuse oneself. Remember, everything we choose we choose for the sake of something else—except happiness, which is an end. So to exert oneself and work for the sake of amusement seems silly and utterly childish."[18]

To Aristotle, happiness comes from people trying to become the best they are capable of becoming. His highest good—*eudaimonia*—has little to do with pleasure but with human flourishing and well-being. Happiness in his view is more akin to the satisfaction one gets from growing as a human being. Accomplishments achieved through great struggle are fulfilling and encouraging. A hedonist, on the other hand, focuses on pleasure and avoiding pain.

Happiness and meaning are both important to well-being. Happiness is related to feeling healthy and good—being a giver rather than a taker in life—and has more to do with satisfying needs and using one's talents and abilities to fulfill a significant goal. A new car may create short-term pleasure but not meaning. A meaningful life is connected to helping others, giving time and effort, and pursuing ideas, missions, or principles larger than oneself.

Self-understanding doesn't come from simply taking a course in joyful living or reading a self-help book. It doesn't happen overnight. Across all demographic groups, Americans find meaning and satisfaction in family, careers, and friendships. Meaning matters.

Pew Research completed a study in which respondents had to describe in their own words what makes life feel meaningful and fulfilling. Spending time with family turned out to be very important. People also cited career and jobs, finances, and friendships, as well as religion. Family, nature, friends, pets, music, and reading were ranked above job or career.

VIKTOR FRANKL AND MEANING

Life is not always peaceful, and goodness does not always prevail. It can go in a multitude of directions. In some cases, dastardly and malicious ways dominate. Death happens and sadness overwhelms. Frustration mounts as ideals are compromised. However, writing a poem brings satisfaction and joy, and tackling an ethical issue and speaking out bring a sense of justice and significance.

History is replete with hardship and totalitarian excesses that are the dark punctuations of brutal and unethical behavior and decisions. And concrete examples exist of positive principles taking precedence and ideals coming into fruition because of the decisions of individuals and the collective greater society.

In many cases, these issues raise the question, "Why am I here?" This has more to do with meaning than happiness or avoidance of pain. It doesn't emanate from egotistical commitments or perspectives or stature or popularity. Meaning in life can be circumvented by ego and its attachments to self-importance. Strong ego tied with corrupt ideas can be very powerful and persuade whole populations to adopt destructive policies. World history presents very vivid examples of that fact.

Popular movies, in their formulaic way, gloss over the difficulty and complexity of confronting life's circumstances and finding understanding and insight. In most films, the character faces a situation, applies himself or herself, experiences a setback, and eventually succeeds in finding a heartwarming solution. In real life, however, lightning doesn't strike, heroes don't ride over the hill, and success and happiness do not always spring to life in ninety minutes. Good does not always prevail over evil, as the Holocaust and other historic tragedies demonstrate.

Neurologist and psychiatrist Viktor Frankl's iconic book, *Man's Search for Meaning*, provides an intense discussion of life and meaning emanating from his time as a concentration camp inmate during the Holocaust. Frankl's experiences in a Nazi concentration camp affected his understanding of reality and the meaning of human existence. During this time, he found that those persons who did not lose a sense of purpose and meaning in life survived much longer than others who lost their way.[19] Even in the most degrading and horrendous circumstances, those individuals who could still see that life had inherent meaning clung to life longer than those who failed to see any meaning in human existence.

Research on alcoholics and drug addicts indicates that 90 and 100 percent, respectively, believe that life is meaningless. When people feel useless, they equate this with leading a meaningless life. Consequently, they leap into activities that numb the pain and deflect them from having to address situations and choose a productive course. They have a sense that they do not matter and, consequently, drug or drink themselves into senselessness, letting their lives fall apart and receding into decadence.

Frankl believes that life has meaning under any and all circumstances, both positive and negative. The main motivation in life is to understand life's significance. Meaninglessness darkens perspective and destroys the imperative to decide and act.

He stated that individuals cannot control what happens to them. However, people are in singular control—have total freedom—over one thing: how they respond to situations and conditions. Every person has the sole power to determine how he or she responds: that determination is singular, personal, and empowering. External forces can take away people's control over many things except their control over their decision of how to react and respond.

Finding meaning in life—the core of the question, Why am I here?—is a primary, not secondary, motivation and requires not passive relaxation or deference to others but striving and struggling for a consequential goal. Frankl states, "Ultimately, a man should not ask what the meaning of his life is, but rather he must recognize that it is he who is asked. In a word, each man is questioned by life; and he can only answer to life by answering for his own life; to life he can only respond by being responsible."[20]

Frankl did not believe that suffering was necessary to find meaning. He thought it was possible to find meaning in spite of suffering, which, at times, was unavoidable. His work cites three ways to discover meaning.

One way is by creating work or doing a deed. Helping others, acting honorably, and ensuring ethical behavior are considerations in decisions. Working to enhance the dignity and viability of others—children, the aged, the poor, the troubled, or the suffering—leads to a sense of significance and meaning.

The second way is by experiencing nature or pursuing great ideas of goodness, truth, and beauty. Principles and ideas open the heart to meaning. Certainly, experiencing another human being, that person's uniqueness and love, can envelop one in the meaning of humanity and life.

The third way is through suffering, which also brings meaning because individuals are challenged to change themselves and adapt to situations. Sometimes the sacrifice one must make in these situations brings greater meaning and appreciation of life.

In raising children, parents pray that their offspring will be happy and free from suffering and pain. As much as that is a caring wish, it is not probable. To some degree, pain and suffering are inevitable. Love, for example, can be the wellspring of pain. When a loved one dies, the broken heart screams of loss, not in a narcissistic way but because of the unselfish love felt for another and the joy that was created in both hearts.

The suffering from that loss remains long after the person's death, and his or her absence is felt for the duration of the lives of those left behind. Goens's poem, "The Presence of Your Absence," illustrates love extending beyond the unexpected death of his daughter:

> The vacant place is always present,
> At the holiday table people talk over the emptiness.
> During quiet times, the place beside me is vacant.
> In times when I need a good word, there is silence.
> When I look to the future, you remain in the past.

> Despite my dreams and desires, absence remains.
> I have come to love the presence of your absence
> For it reminds me of my deep love for you
> And the place in my heart where you live
> Always there—present and forever
> In the reality of your absence.

Hearts break because of the joy of love. Pain, in many cases, has its foundation in life's joys and increases our capacity to better understand the joy and hope we experience either with others or simply in our quiet moments, doing the things we love.

Getting through suffering and pain is what people have to do, and it isn't easy. Every individual at one time or another must face internal sadness that others cannot erase. Loss, however, does bring people together as individuals reach out in concern and empathy. While others cannot erase or eliminate suffering, they understand its power from their own experience and compassion. Suffering teaches humility and the fact that connections to others are a valuable part of an individual's wholeness. It teaches compassion and brings people down from preconceived perches to greater understanding of self, others, and life.

With suffering comes uncertainty. With a loss of any kind, the picture of life and of those remaining looks different. A cornerstone—friend, parent, mentor, lover—is missing. But through that fear, new perspectives unfold and new beginnings emerge.

Instead of simply trying to be happy and living a life others expect, people must become attached to something greater than themselves and want to apply their strengths to something meaningful, not just trivial or lucrative pursuits.

Fred Kofman identifies "four pillars" that intrinsically motivate people in pursuing something "greater":

- Purpose: significance, meaning, impact, service, and self-transcendence
- Principles: integrity, ethics, morality, goodness, truth, and dignity
- People: belonging, connection, community, recognition, respect, and praise
- Freedom: creativity, achievement, learning, and self-mastery[21]

In responding to the question, "Why am I here?" people must look inward and determine the values on which they stand, what behavior makes them true to themselves, and what actions will be honorable to their efforts regardless of whether they are successful or not.

Love, wisdom, courage, justice, and temperance are qualities of character that build relationships with others and establish a framework for what is meaningful and how to address circumstances. Meaningful actions are right, justifiable, and good. Narcissistic deceit and cheating may prevail at times, but they do not create meaning, and they ultimately diminish character and self-worth.

What one really leaves behind is a sense of oneself—one's character and ethos. People remember the "self" that highlights an individual's persona.

John Gardner specifically defined how to find meaning in life. He stated,

> Meaning is not something you stumble across, like the answer to a riddle or the prize in a treasure hunt. Meaning is something you build into your life. You build it out of your past, out of your affections and loyalties, out of the experience of humankind as it is passed on to you, out of your talent and understanding, out of the things you believe in, out of the things and people you love, out of the values for which you are willing to sacrifice something. The ingredients are there. You are the only one who can put them together into that unique pattern that will be your life. Let it be a life that has dignity and meaning for you. If it does, then the particular balance of success or failure—as the world measures success or failure—is of less account. [22]

Philosophers and other learned people are focused on life. Nietzsche, in his meditation on "Schopenhauer as Educator," stated, "We must give a responsible account of our existence before our own selves; it follows that we must wish to be real helmsmen of this life rather than allowing it to become thoughtless and arbitrary. One must take a somewhat mischievous and dangerous attitude towards existence, especially since one will always lose it in the end, however poorly or well things may turn out." [23]

Parker Palmer illustrated the purpose of life very simply when he wrote, "No one ever died saying, 'I'm so glad for the self-centered, self-

serving, and self-protective life that I lived.' Offer yourself to the
world—your energies, your gifts, your visions, your spirit—with open-
hearted generosity."[24] To do so, a person must have a clear sense of self
and know where and how he or she stands.

Independent

He was solitary
Independent they say
But not lonely.
Simply living in comfort
Within himself and his place.
The pack runs off on missions of conformity
While he begins alone, apart
Howling an independent tune.
He stands up when the others
Silently stand down.
Cursing the darkness to him
Is not without virtue.
He lives within himself
Seemingly aloof to others
But totally open
To ideas and perspectives.
On the surface he seems hard
Shading the soft core
Of his soulful comfort
And the humility of age.
He was himself.

WHAT TO REMEMBER

- Growing into adulthood raises very clearly the question, "Why am I here?" and issues of pragmatism, philosophy, and meaning.
- Each generation's perspectives and perceptions are formed, in part, because of its members' parents and education but also because of the social and economic context in which they were raised.
- Some countries and societies confront the issue of decadence of identity based on narcissism, nihilism, and collectivism, among others, along with pressures to conform.

- Individualism is necessary to be able to realize one's own potential based on strong values, principles, and beliefs.
- Happiness emanates from the choices people make in fulfilling their values and principles.
- Under any and all circumstances, each individual is totally free to determine how to respond to the circumstances.
- Pain and suffering are part of life: everyone at some time or another experiences loss, but pursuing something greater than self-interest as a response to pain can bring meaning.

NOTES

1. Palmer, Parker J., *Let Your Life Speak* (San Francisco: Jossey-Bass Publishers, 2000), 7.

2. Leary, Mark R., ed., *Handbook for Self and Identity* (New York: Guilford Press, 2011), 71–76, Kindle.

3. Pew Research Center, "How Millennials Today Compare with Their Grandparents 50 Years Ago," March 16, 2018, http://www.pewresearch.org/fact-tank/2018/03/16/how-millennials-compare-with-their-grandparents/.

4. Pew Research Center, "The Generation Gap in American Politics," March 1, 2018, http://assets.pewresearch.org/wp-content/uploads/sites/5/2018/03/01122435/03-01-18-Generations-release.pdf.

5. Solly, Meilan, "US Life Expectancy Drops for Third Year in a Row, Reflecting Rising Drug Overdoses, Suicides," *Smithsonian*, December 3, 2018, https://www.smithsonianmag.com/smart-news/us-life-expectancy-drops-third-year-row-reflecting-rising-drug-overdose-suicide-rates-180970942/.

6. Glubb, Sir John, "The Fate of Empires and Search for Survival," 1976, http://people.uncw.edu/kozloffm/glubb.pdf.

7. LaFlaur, Mark, "The Writing Life," *Los Angeles Times*, May 21, 2000, http://articles.latimes.com/2000/may/21/books/bk-32271.

8. LaFlaur, "Writing Life."

9. "In Depth: Jacques Barzun," *Booktv*, C-Span2, May 6, 2001, https://www.youtube.com/watch?v=Nbpg0fqfL1w.

10. Wheatley, Margaret J., *Who Do We Choose to Be?* (San Francisco: Berrett-Koehler Publishers, 2017), 35, Kindle.

11. Wheatley, *Who Do We Choose to Be?*, 65.

12. Gardner, John W., *Self Renewal: The Individual and the Innovative Society* (New York: Norton and Company, 1981), 36.

13. Moore, Thomas. *Care of the Soul* (New York: HarperPerennial, 1992), 5.

14. Wheatley, *Who Do We Choose to Be?*, 275.

15. Carlin, George, *Last Words* (New York: Simon & Schuster, 2009), 284, Kindle.

16. Fromm, Erich, *To Have or to Be* (New York: Continuum, 2003), 110.

17. Bonhoeffer, Dietrich, *Letters and Papers from Prison* (New York: Touchstone, 1977), 419.

18. O'Toole, James, *Creating the Good Life* (New York: Rodale Publishers, 2005), 42.

19. Frankl, Viktor E., *Man's Search for Meaning* (Boston: Beacon Press, 2006), 140–43, Kindle.

20. Frankl, *Man's Search for Meaning*, 109.

21. Kofman, Fred, *The Meaning Revolution* (New York: Crown Publishing Group, 2018), 121–27, Kindle.

22. Gardner, John, *Living, Leading and the American Dream* (San Francisco: Jossey-Bass, 2003), 53.

23. Pellerin, Daniel, trans., "Schopenhauer as Educator," 2014, 3.

24. Palmer, Parker J., *On the Brink of Everything* (Oakland, CA: Berrett-Koehler Publishers, 2018), 45.

7

HOCKEY, BUTTERFLIES, AND LIFE

To venture causes anxiety, but not to venture is to lose oneself. . . .
And to venture in the highest is precisely to be conscious of oneself.
—Soren Kierkegaard

Cartoonist and writer Allen Saunders stated, "Life is what happens to us while we're making other plans." Even in seemingly quiet and stable times, surprising twists and turns erupt. Life is not an exercise in engineering.

Change is unabating but not always predictable or obvious. Individuals can prepare for it, but they cannot control the seemingly constant state of disequilibrium that sometimes borders on chaos. Nothing is ever static. Inexplicable events happen. Rational plans and a sense of stability are waylaid. Chaos seems to reign in both internal and external worlds. Things are in flux, sometimes very subtly, and at other times with unexpected power and swiftness.

Ups and downs and gains and losses sometimes occur simultaneously. The plateau of certainty evaporates, and the terrain transforms into peaks of joy or valleys of loss. At times, people glide gently through, and at other times they crash into difficult conditions—some minor and others overwhelmingly deep and hard.

At times, good fortune shines simply because individuals happen to be in the right place at the right time. Through seemingly serendipitous events, they meet their lifetime partner in an unanticipated spot at an unplanned time or they make an important career contact at a coffee shop through a random conversation. But then a difficult twist of fate occurs, and they face a health emergency, the loss of a job, an errant driver crashing into them, or an unexpected death.

"The best laid plans"—an old, familiar phrase—get derailed in the nonlinear world, which is not a fixed state and does not always operate like clockwork and with cause-and-effect precision. Plans sputter and flop, and the unexpected happens.

In this type of world, improvising is a great asset. However, ironically, improvisation and life are seldom mentioned in the same breath. In reality, issues crop up and decisions must be made in the moment, without time for deep reflection. In such decision-making situations, principles and values matter, because every choice may carry unintended and unforeseen consequences.

HOCKEY AND BUTTERFLIES

Chaos theory is at work. While gravity, for example, is predictable, there are nonlinear things in life that are difficult to foresee or control. The weather is a chaotic system, not always easy to forecast and certainly not controllable. The economy, stock market, and society are also chaotic systems. Sometimes, small and unexpected changes bring significant transformations.

A grandfather sat with his grandson and turned on the television to watch the hockey game that was about to start. The grandfather looked his grandson in the eye and said, "You know, Eddie, life is like a hockey game."

His twelve-year-old grandson looked at him quizzically, wondering, What's this conversation about?

"I know what you're thinking, but it's not simply scoring goals, body checking, or being sent to the penalty box," his grandfather chuckled. "It's a bit more subtle than that. Sometimes you win, sometimes you lose, and occasionally you tie."

"A hockey game, huh. Life is a game?" Eddie questioned.

"No, it can be fun, but it's about what happens in a game, like in hockey or any other team sport: there are surprising things that happen. Remember the Wayne Gretzky quote I read to you. He was one of the best, if not *the* best, hockey player ever to play the game. But he had a little different perspective than many other players who were good."

His grandfather picked up a book from the pile by his chair and opened it.

"This is what Gretzky said: 'A good hockey player plays where the puck is. A great hockey player plays where the puck is going to be.' He also said, 'I skate to where the puck is going to be, not to where it has been.' There is a lot of wisdom in these comments relating to life, Eddie."

"I know what that means in a hockey game, Grandpa, but I don't get what it means in life."

"Well, in life you have to understand that change is happening—some of it subtle—and anticipate where it is going so that you can deal with it and make the most of it. In life, like in a hockey game, you play and figure out what you have to do to make a play and win the game. Sometimes, the change is not noticeable right away. Six players on each side making small moves alter the game's dynamics. You don't always know what may happen next."

"Yeah, my coach says we have to keep our heads up, see what's happening, and react," Eddie commented.

"You know why he said that?"

"So I don't get hit?"

"That's one reason. There's one more," his grandfather said. "Butter-flies."

"C'mon, Grandpa! Butterflies . . . in a hockey game? Wait 'til I tell my coach," Eddie laughed.

"Yes, this sounds crazy. Butterflies in hockey, football, or basketball games!"

In hockey games and other sports, Eddie's grandfather is right. Chaos, certainly disorder, seems constant and pervasive. Everyone, at one time or another, has experienced the "butterfly effect." In simple language, it's explained this way: a butterfly flapping its wings in Asia causes a hurricane in the Atlantic. In other words, small and muted changes or events can create significant and complex results.

"Eddie, you know changes are happening in a game, but they are not always easily seen. That's what makes it interesting and exciting. And, remember, you don't always have to score a goal to be a great player," the grandfather commented. "By the way, when's your next game? I'll come and watch. Don't forget—keep your head up and watch for the butterflies," he laughed.

Eddie's grandfather was using the metaphor of a hockey game to explain that beneath the disorder of the game, players on each team continually self-organize and adjust their game to competing players and changing situations. The connections and interrelationships between team members and opposing players influence each individual player's performance as well as the entire teams.

Getting back to the sports metaphor, each individual player in the hockey game experiences and exhibits varying levels of exhaustion, pressure, or focus. Metaphorically each player is a small system, and his or her individual muscle fatigue and strain and break in concentration affect the dynamics of the play and other players and ultimately determine whether the team wins or loses. Some of these individual factors are not evident to the crowd, coach, or teammates.

While things seem out of control, they are not because teams consistently self-organize and alter their strategy or methods. "The term 'order' does not refer to characteristics such as quiet, calm, or good, but refers instead to a self-organizing pattern, shape, or structure."[1] Strategic structures, individual adjustments, and intangible commitments shape order in the chaos.

Eddie's grandfather had an inkling of chaos theory and the butterfly effect. "A small change in the initial conditions of one system multiply upward, expanding into larger and larger systems, changing conditions all along the way, eventually causing unexpected consequences on a broader level sometime in the future."[2]

SELF-ORGANIZATION

Self-organization is important in all facets of life as things subtly unfold or crash into being. Chaos brings about change in nature and life, including society. People have to get information and adjust.

Individuals or groups self-organize if they can get feedback and insight about what is occurring and then develop foresight about what can or may arise. Getting feedback and being conscious of what is occurring individually and collectively can alter perspective; recognition about what has to be done to address the change develops.

In these chaotic systems, nonlinear thinking and the use of intuition and intellectual understanding are necessary to recognize the long-term changes that are occurring. People in severed relationships will indicate, "I just made a small comment, and all hell broke loose and eventually that was the seed that destroyed our relationship."

Rigidly sticking to plans in such a dynamic environment is a recipe for difficulty and/or failure. Emotional, nonlinear, nonquantifiable, and hidden forces derail the best of plans. What is manifest is not the problem. It is what is emerging that creates havoc for plans. Chaos prevails and is a part of all open social systems—life itself is an open system.

In Sir Isaac Newton's sixteenth-century world, part-to-whole thinking and linear logic reigned. The "machinery" of managing life would succeed because everyone would do their "part" and respond as anticipated. But the world is not as Newton thought it was; the universe is not like a machine that runs like a clock. It is full of hidden and interconnected fields and forces that cannot be seen or measured, affecting people and plans. Willpower, determination, and other emotions are intangible forces that can produce dramatic change and outcomes.

People desire life to emerge like a rational decision-making plan; once they identify goals, examine alternatives, review pluses and minuses, select and implement a strategy, and monitor and evaluate outcomes, the life they desire will play out. Their aim is to make logically sound decisions based on an orderly path of identifying problems, determining solutions, and getting results.

Sometimes this works. Many organizations and corporations are designed on this premise but not without problems. Technology since the 1990s has changed life dramatically for individuals and corporations and will continue to do so. While technology has brought improvement, it has also brought privacy and information concerns as well as emotional and addiction issues. The evolution of jobs and work has been dramatic and will continue to be so into the future.

All people face two types of decisions. First, there are substantive decisions, which concern destinations: the desired goals and objectives, the "whats" and "whys" of what they want or need. Second, there are tactical or strategic decisions, which involve the processes for and approaches to achieving those goals and objectives, the "hows" people employ to attain the "whys" and "whats" of success.

Successful people are aware of the obvious and subtle dynamics of situations. They learn and develop the insight and foresight to read observable situations, and they understand the invisible fields and forces at play. They know when to change course to reach a goal and when to be creative and break with convention, ethically and with integrity, to be successful. Steering the course to a successful life requires ingenuity and improvisation.

THINKING ANEW: TANGIBLES AND INTANGIBLES

Everyone thinks about the future, but how they think and what they think affects their choices in confronting it. Einstein stated, "The world we have created is a product of our way of thinking." If we think differently, viewpoints and approaches change; in other words, the world does not operate like a machine.

Today, self-organization and chaos theory have altered thinking about how the world or relationships operate. Life is more fluid, and people and organizations self-organize: they learn and adapt to chaos and change. As such, relationships are critically important, and ethics and values matter because they influence personal and organizational behavior. Thought creates invisible fields that influence how people react. A key is seeing the world as not simply made up of tangible things but also of relationships, energy, and possibilities, as well as fields.[3] Thought fields produce energy and focus along with passion and commitment.

Commitment, an intangible gift, according to Joseph Jaworski, can direct decisions and behavior: "When we are in a state of commitment and surrender, we begin to experience what is sometimes called synchronicity."[4] Synchronicity is not magical or mystical. C. J. Jung defined synchronicity as "a meaningful coincidence of two or more events, where something other than the probability of chance is involved."[5]

Many people have had the experience of coincidence where they, in a surprising and timely manner, meet people, achieve things, or obtain resources essential to them. "The people who come to you are the very people you need in relation to your commitment. Doors open, a sense of flow develops, and you find you are acting in a coherent field of people who may not even be aware of one another."[6]

Fields—gravity is one obvious example—are all around; energy, both personal and universal, is powerful. In some cases, these fields cannot be measured. They can be observed as people unify and work together as one, with flow, inspiration, and personal commitment.

Personal energy, commitment, meaning, and presence are all at play. They have to do with an individual's "being." Each individual must trust his or her purpose and destiny and work toward them; things will unfold as people see themselves connected to the greater universe and to one another. People come to understand what they were meant to do, and they find what is significant and purposeful.

Several traps exist that cause people to fall back into old patterns instead of moving ahead.[7] One is a trap of responsibility: the feeling of being indispensable and responsible for everything and others at all times. Falling back in meeting others' expectations becomes overwhelming, and therefore, protecting the status quo becomes dominant. This is a trap because individuals cannot control everything.

A second trap is one of dependence, where individuals feel dependent on others and don't wish to offend them by acting independently. This emanates from a sense of uncertainty, inadequacy, and unworthiness. Individuals become dependent on old plans and scenarios because of fearing new or different ways to get things done.

A third trap is overactivity: feverishly working to get things done. Focusing on the past, unimportant details, and old baggage curtails following through on important things. Falling out of balance occurs, becoming bogged down in minutia, and managing but not creating is the result.

People must overcome their fear of what others think and expect. Reflection and listening to their "inner voice" are necessary. Sometimes, people feel they are in "the zone" because their focus, and the energy from that focus, helps them progress and make connections. Thinking produces energy, but the old baggage of mistakes, failure, misunderstandings, and toxic relationships must be dumped to move forward.

EMOTIONAL INTELLIGENCE

Intelligence is important and respected in our society. Brains matter, and the media highlight those with intellectual skills and abilities. However, there are very smart people who cannot succeed. They are intelligent but vacuous. The issue may be their lack of emotional intelligence. People in that category may know content but lack self-understanding and social skills. Being able to read others and building positive relations are not skills that are automatically developed by someone who is academically brilliant.

Daniel Goleman's book *Emotional Intelligence*, specifically addresses why emotional intelligence is important for professional, social, and interpersonal aspects of life. There are several components: three have to do with personal abilities, and two concern relationships with others.[8]

One critical skill is self-awareness, which involves an introspective examination of one's drives, values, strengths, and weaknesses. All of these affect relationships with others. Self-understanding has to do with self-confidence and realizing the impact of moods on self and others.

Despite people thinking they are always making rational decisions, emotion plays a part. Unconscious bias actually filters into how individuals perceive things. The mind, which is not synonymous with the brain, is at work, which involves an individual's total experience and cognitive, emotional, physical, and spiritual self.

An aspect of emotional intelligence includes knowing one's emotions and state of mind and managing them. Recognizing feelings and dealing with them appropriately are important and involve coping with the impact of other people's emotions. Developing the knowledge, attitudes, and skills necessary to manage one's feelings is necessary to establish positive relationships and demonstrate caring and concern for others, to make responsible decisions, and to handle challenging and uncomfortable situations.

In essence, "the emotional skills include self-awareness: identifying, expressing, and managing feelings; impulse control and delaying gratification; and handling stress and anxiety. A key ability in impulse control is knowing the difference between feelings and actions, and learning to make better emotional decisions by first controlling impulse to act, then identifying alternative actions and their consequences before acting."[9]

Individuals have to discern and react to situations and circumstances appropriately. Their perceptions of others are important because they are framed, in part, by individual interactions and reactions to them. Understanding how others relate to oneself is important. Sometimes, what people know about themselves is unknown to others, and conversely what others may know about an individual is unknown to that individual.

Mindfulness is important to focusing, concentrating, and becoming fully engaged in relationships and work. Mindfulness, the starting point of self-awareness, has two key qualities: focus and awareness.[10] Focus simply is the ability to be single-minded in what one does in order to create awareness of what is happening in one's mind moment to moment. This helps one to pause and make conscious and deliberative choices. Understanding what is happening encourages self-understanding.

Self-understanding leads in turn to being able to self-regulate by controlling impulses that negatively impact, discourage, or disrupt others. Basically, that means suspending judgments, and thinking before acting. Doing so builds up one's integrity and increases trustworthiness—being able to demonstrate to others that one will not recoil or go off unhinged in the heat of the moment. Ambiguity exists in life, and being comfortable with it is necessary. Things are not always clear; however, they can become understandable with collective thought, time, and dialogue.

Another aspect of emotional intelligence is motivation. People commit to working on worthy causes and noble ideas, even failure will not deter them. Their desire to achieve becomes contagious. Coercion doesn't work—it only creates animosity—but dedication does.

Emotional intelligence includes not only self-awareness, self-regulation, and motivation but also empathy, the ability to understand other's emotional makeup and position. Being able to comprehend the emotional tenor of others is essential. Sensitivity along gender, race, and cultural lines builds understanding and cooperation. Put another way, treating others according to their emotional makeup creates an environment that is sensitive, which demonstrates respect to others and understanding, which are required to build relationships and develop talent.

One final component of emotional intelligence, social skill, is required in finding common ground, cooperation, and positive work relationships, which bring about better teamwork on mutual goals and on confronting change.[11] Being persuasive with others in a positive sense, and being able to appeal to people's "better angels," can tie people together in common purpose.

Technical ability devoid of social intelligence is not effective. Doing the chores and meeting responsibilities may get things done. But families, work groups, and social groups are about more than getting tasks completed. They require two major intelligences—self-understanding and social understanding—to motivate them. Cognitive intelligence matters, but emotional intelligence enables the collective intelligence of others to pursue meaningful purposes.

The influence of parents and others may initially be significant in directing a person's life path, but parents and others are not always a major influence as individuals mature and find their own way. External circumstances, beyond family, impact perspectives and aspirations; some emanate from newer relationships and others from social, political, and cultural events. All these situations and circumstances define individuals' viewpoints and the contexts they confront.

A person's life course includes socially defined events and roles over time and in different phases and may not occur in a particular order. Several factors are involved, including social-historical events, geographical location, timing, social ties, personal control, and how the past shapes the future.

People create their own life by the choices and actions they take, but these choices may be influenced by the personal and social-historical events they experience. Having a thoughtful, proactive, and controlled approach to decisions is important, as decision-making goes on throughout all stages of life.

IMPROVISATION AND LIFE

As much as people may desire it to be, life is not an assured path to preferred outcomes where victory shines and failures are nonexistent. Generally, people wish to paint a rosy scenario of life. Optimists, not pessimists, shine. Realists, however, understand that more diverse experience, while difficult at times, may also bring opportunity and learning.

Life advances and expected and unexpected things happen at prescribed as well as unexpected times. Problems arise; trying to avoid them usually brings about additional, sometimes larger, issues. Even if people have clear pictures of what they want in life, they may not have sufficient support or resources to get there. Barriers exist: some based on factors of race, gender, ethnicity and some on access and/or knowledge of systems and traditions.

Successful people are aware of the obvious and subtle dynamics of situations. They learn and know through information and intuition, develop the insight and foresight to read observable situations, and understand the invisible fields and forces at play. They know when to change course to reach a goal and when to be creative and break with convention ethically and with integrity to be successful. Steering the course to success may require ingenuity and improvisation.

Improvisation generally affects tactical decisions on how to reach goals and maintain integrity. Noble goals are achieved because of the insight of individuals to read situations and respond tactically in effective and constructive ways. Many strategic decisions involve the intangibles of organizational life and the intuitive ways of knowing and understanding.

Several questions about improvising arise. First, does improvising create unexpected consequences that can reap great advantages? Unanticipated opportunities may surface because a person takes a creative or unexpected course. These opportunities may open doors to achievement that were not evident before.

Second, does improvising destroy the individual's integrity? Means do not justify ends. Selling out values and principles to achieve a goal does irreparable harm and eventually devastates the value-driven behavior necessary for success.

Third, does improvising produce learning and provide a new or unique slant on an issue, causing individuals to think differently? People learn and incorporate new ways to achieve goals or to relate to each other differently because improvisation shows new possibilities and increases the capacity of people and organizations.

Through improvising, people sometimes learn that they can cut steps out of a process and still achieve their goals. Improvisation can speed up action, and when time and resources are limited, this can be a great advantage.

The events and directions of life open choices and provide perspective—maybe even wisdom. Awareness can blossom into knowledge and competence, and hopefully, each success or disappointment provides insight into a sense of self and identity. Then life, as one looks back on it, makes sense, and individual purpose and meaning become clearer.

Magical Moments

Magical moments spring to life
On the wings of a nighthawk
Floating high, sifting the wind
Through its wings
They come through the solitary
Howl piercing through the trees of a
Lone coyote greeting the night.
The magic glows in the eyes
Of neighbors sharing the quiet
Brotherhood of nature.
Magical moments spark to life
In ways unexpected, untouched
By the plastic hands of lives
Invented in our mind.

WHAT TO REMEMBER

- In life, chaos and self-organizing systems are at play that alter circumstances and bring about change.
- Self-organization is necessary for individuals to address changing dynamics and circumstances.
- Emotional intelligence concerns self-awareness, self-regulation, motivation, empathy, and social skill.
- People require social intelligence, as well as cognitive intelligence, to work through life. Understanding develops through self-awareness of moods and emotions.
- Fields, energy, and synchronicity are present in all aspects of life and produce change.
- A person's life course and generational experiences affect perceptions and opinions.
- Improvisation is important in life and concerns tactical decisions to reach goals and objectives. Principles form the foundation for improvisation.

NOTES

1. Sanders, T. Irene, *Strategic Thinking and the New Science* (New York: The Free Press, 1998), 70.

2. Sanders, *Strategic Thinking and the New Science*, 57.

3. Wheatley, Margaret, *Leadership and the New Science* (San Francisco: Berrett-Koehler Publishers, 1999), 13–14.

4. Jaworski, Joseph, *Synchronicity: The Inner Path of Leadership* (San Francisco: Berrett-Koehler Publishers, 1996), 14.

5. Jaworski, *Synchronicity*, 88.

6. Jaworski, *Synchronicity*, 184–85.

7. Jaworski, *Synchronicity*, 121.

8. Goleman, Daniel, "What Makes a Leader?" *Harvard Business Review* (November–December 1998): 7–21.

9. Goleman, Daniel, *Emotional Intelligence: Why It Can Matter More Than IQ* (New York: Random House, 2012), 259, Kindle.

10. Hougaard, Rasmus, and Carter, Jacqueline, "The Mindful Leader," *Rotman Management* (Fall 2018): 33–37.

11. Goleman, "What Makes a Leader?"

8

EDUCATION AND SELF

Education must not simply teach work—it must teach Life.
—W. E. B. Du Bois

I have no special talent. I am only passionately curious.
—Albert Einstein

Students face thousands of questions as they go through school. Some are matters of recall of facts and figures, and others may concern higher-order questions of analysis and evaluation. The assumption is that by studying and mastering academic content in math, science, English, social studies, and other subjects, students will gain self-understanding and be able to find their true selves and be productive citizens.

Education, from its inception in the United States, was geared to citizenship, governance, and the needs of society. A nation founded on explicit ideals and principles and not royal privilege, divine right, or totalitarian autocracy requires educated citizens to comprehend those ideals and values and actively engage in self-government. Discerning what is in harmony with from what is contrary to the nation's tenets is vital in a nation that encourages free speech, debate, and active participation in expressing opinions through the ballot.

Another dimension of education is the assumption that if students obtain the skills, knowledge, and attitude necessary to earn a living and become active citizens, they will discover a sense of self. Intellectual prowess can be measured in most content areas, but attitudes are observed in visible behavior. Education must move beyond simple academic prowess to the deeper understanding of principles, ethics, and standards and their impact on finding a sense of self and leading a good life.

FORGOTTEN QUESTIONS: THE SELF

In school, children think about themselves and wonder what the future holds. These two ponderings are basic at home, at work, or in society. Coming to grips with themselves—heart, mind, and soul—involves discovering their fundamental nature. No matter how capable one is academically—no matter the extent of one's education or training—understanding self is essential in life's journey.

Each person is distinctive, and each life is one-of-a-kind and invaluable. Individuals are confronted with understanding who they are and why they exist. They are not easy questions, and they seldom prompt easy answers. People can gain the highest academic standing possible and still not be able to answer these basic questions or find the happiness that comes with meaning and purpose. No classes or tests exist about whether one has self-understanding and a mature self-concept.

Education—academic or otherwise—may not provide all the answers, but it may, to use colloquialisms, open doors or turn on lights to understanding and insight. Instructional strategies are not the only means to get an education. Technology is a tool but not an answer in uncovering the true self, because technology has no human element; it reflects binary algorithms and provides access to information. Wisdom is not gained through algorithmic research or by earning diplomas and degrees. Wisdom is much more than recall and retention and is key to living a life of character.

In the reality of life people learn, not only in school but also from experiences and episodes that go into making the total person, not only their cognitive abilities but also ways to nourish their hearts and souls. Certainly, formal education is invaluable, providing it helps people understand life and the ethics and principles that make families and society noble and enables people to freely develop their lives, talents, and passions.

Education comes in many forms. Schooling provides a backdrop for learning, particularly for the mastering of content and skills. In addition, it can awaken interests and talents that turn into true passions that can direct one's life.

Life presents other ways to educate as well; they are not necessarily pleasant and easy, but they are powerful and poignant. Hardships and suffering are powerful teachers. Destiny in terms of losses or crises often sets up the opportunity for introspection and an awakening of one's values and purpose. The pain one feels in moments of loss may open the doors to understanding life and what is primary and valuable. These times are not easy, but demanding battles can lead to a greater understanding of purpose, commitment, and joy.

In reality, although everyone would like their children, among others, to not have to face them, distress and hardship are evident in everyone's life. They can open people's eyes and lead them to commit to pursuing life to the fullest, with the realization that doing so requires more than a veneer of materialistic pleasure. The importance of bonds with others far exceeds plastic gratification.

In times of suffering, solitude is a path to greater understanding. Being with oneself and feeling loss or pain (or success and achievement, in better times) can lead to insight and commitment. Being alone can be difficult. People try to escape solitude and seek redress with others, fearing the unknown, failure, or isolation. But the inner voice awakens in solitude, away from the cacophony of daily life. A quiet mind allows inner feelings to be heard and understood. Business and social interactions divert the ability to sit with oneself and reflect. Nature frequently provides a good respite in which to enter solitude and reflect.

TEACHERS—POLESTARS

A major aspect of education, often unnoticed, is the impact of mentors—teachers and others. Individual relationships with mentors can exceed content or academic goals by providing wise feedback and support to individuals. Confidence and courage are often the result of these relationships.

Polestars—those individuals who provide guiding principles to help others look inward and find themselves—render to individuals care and understanding that can be life-changing. A polestar is selected by an individual in need, not chosen for the individual by others or by technology, because of personal, emotional relationships and trust developed between the two people.

Significant teachers and others create deep connections, mentoring and nurturing children so that they rise to be their best. This entails, at times, telling them in a caring way the difficult truths they need to hear in order to be the people they desire to be. This includes feedback not only about their classwork but also about their attitudes, behavior, and perspectives. This feedback causes students to self-reflect about them-*selves*. Principled and ethical, mentors provide honest and strong guidance and insight even if not what students may want to hear, but they do it in a caring and loving way to help students achieve their goals.

Teachers cultivate the originality and understanding of students' being and liberate the spirit within them. They help students see who they are and what they can become. In many cases, teachers clarify by highlighting students' strengths and removing other issues that disrupt students' ability to pursue their calling and achieve their potential. Educators shed light and provide encouraging comfort and insight that cause students to understand what they should sustain and improve.

The impact of a polestar may not be felt immediately. Sometimes a teacher's impact is understood only in retrospect and with the reflection of time. Significance is not measured on a value-added test or by an evaluator viewing classroom practices or lesson plans. Learning does not happen in equal installments that come through a caring relationship. Research shows that positive relationships with adults who provide support are a critical factor in helping children understand themselves.

Classrooms at all education levels are not unemotional cubicles of reason. In actuality they are emotional places with connections with teachers, colleagues, and, certainly, content and learning. Students with significant teachers have an emotional connection based around care, understanding, and patience. In addition, those teachers are examples of moral standards and principles.

Teachers provide emotional support and help students master difficult content and skills. Students must self-reflect on their abilities and commit to pursuing their creativity and uniqueness. Having a teacher "believe in you" is a powerful force in finding the self that is to be unveiled.

Polestars help individuals clarify and pursue purpose and personal significance in life. Finding purpose takes effort, thoughtfulness, scholarly understanding, and passion. Ultimately, that is the philosophical goal of education.

Peter Senge commented that "everyone deserves an education that is about their own development as a human being. The purpose of an education is for me to become me—in the context of the society that I live, so I can truly contribute to my society."[1]

Knowing oneself brings meaning beyond the ability to achieve status or fiscal success. Finding meaning and a calling crosses all sectors of life: personal, social, economic, and philosophical. Contributing to causes beyond oneself promotes both individual and collective well-being. A good life is the result of self-understanding and relationships with others and the application of one's talent, potential, and inner voice.

Education is more than simply completing tasks and assignments. In actuality, it is about "being." People are not human doings; they are beings. Human beings must find their true selves through a developmental process of introspection, self-discovery, and assessment of failures and successes. Instrumental aspects of this process are values, passions, and thought patterns.

SALMON RUNS

In a democracy, independent thinking and thinkers are absolutely indispensable, otherwise individuals get lost in social media's advertising, which is concerned with what is fashionable and details socially acceptable images and styles.

Today, children are socially engaged. Facebook's lamentable distortion of the term *friend* reflects the narcissistic desire by some to be noticed—to garner more and more so-called friends even as they sit in isolation in front of a screen. Certainly "selfies" are another conceited means to gain attention and be acknowledged.

William Deresiewicz identified the "salmon run" in his study of students at elite colleges. These students have been successful at achieving excellent grades, recognition, trophies, and other accolades. By these measures, they are at the top of their classes.

The "salmon run" was described by one of Deresiewicz's former students as a kind of conveyor belt in which "the operative principle is known as triangular desire: wanting something because you see that other people want it and assume that it must be valuable." He names fear as a driving force that "lies behind the façade of serene achievement that elite college students learn to show to the world."[2] Many of the students have never experienced failure: not succeeding is terrifying to them.

The result is that, deterred by the possibility of failure, students have an aversion to risk. Falling short is not in their life's equation. "Experimenting, exploring, discovering new ways to look at the world as well as new capacities within yourself—the things a college education is supposed to be about—fall by the wayside. Nobody wants to let any of the dozen balls they're juggling drop; nobody wants to lag behind in the credentials race."[3] In this view, reputation and success must be maintained and are the markers of who the students are as individuals. They stick to courses and subjects they know well rather than step off the curb and risk a new direction.

What they miss is the opportunity to build a sense of self, which is necessary for living life in all its phases. The self must be developed; it is not premade. A sense of "this is who I am and what I stand for" is buried by fear and anxiety, which closes doors to new perspectives, opportunities, and encounters. Maintaining an elite image, not exploring something different, is the motivation. Reputation, not learning, is the goal.

Education in reality should be about ventures and challenges. After all, school provides students with the ability to stretch themselves in a safe and understanding context. Failure is an option, one that provides a challenge that supersedes one's current skills and abilities. From failure, students learn not only cognitive and technical knowledge but also emotional fortitude and understanding, which are essential to an uncertain and evolving future.

Taking the sure road with a satisfying certainty does nothing to help students traverse change, loss, or failure. Emotionally soothing one's ego weakens the spirit when life's difficulties arise, as surely they will. After all, many things, including life itself, are uncertain. While not always pleasant, working through failure can sharpen self-understanding and develop creative insights.

SELF AND CALLING

Near the end of life, people look back and some have regrets. A major regret is not having had the courage to live their lives true to themselves. Perhaps they find that having lived to meet other's expectations leaves them hollow, that there have been no second chances, and each choice made in response to situations has been, in the end, their personal decision. No one else is to blame.

Becoming a unique self comes with having a sense of soul, a total being, with moral, emotional, sensual, and intellectual feelings. "The heart feels . . . and the intelligence is educated by reflecting on that feeling. Everyone is born with a mind, but it is only through this act of introspection, of self-examination, of establishing communication between the mind and the heart, the mind and experience, that you become an individual, a unique being—a soul. And that is what it means to develop a self."[4]

Discovering a sense of self comes from introspection; experience with art, music, and literature; examining philosophical ideas, values, and principles; understanding scientific thinking; and feeling the love and affection that come through human interaction.

The foundation for all of this is one's beliefs and attitudes, which determine how one chooses to live and interact. A sense of soul—of being—in life comes as individuals face life's pain, elation, and travails and expand themselves both through success and failure.

One's truth and self ultimately involve living with integrity to one's own beliefs and values and not to the external conceptions and desires of others. As the saying goes, "You only have one life to live." Finding one's way is a true gift—a gift that leads to purpose.

Another gift is finding a vocation. To some, vocation raises the specter of a job or employment. But the Latin root of *vocation* means "calling," which chooses you and not vice versa.[5] A calling becomes evident when individuals free themselves and open their minds and hearts to what they really are passionate about, freeing themselves from others' aspirations. Only the individual can discover his or her calling; no one can do it for another person.

Calling has implications for self-actualization and resolve. In many cases, students try to live a life that someone else already lived. The expectations of others or false expectations that have been implanted in their minds deter individuals from taking a path that calls from within—from their heart, mind, and soul.

Discovering one's calling requires "listening to the voice of your life."[6] Basically, that means understanding one's true self and gaining insight into one's mission, which happens through reflection on life's experiences of all stripes. Finding an inner sense and passion is a gift.

Imagination as well as moral and ethical purpose calls one to move ahead with what one's mind and character demands. Courage is required for self-expression and freedom from what others think or desire. A calling unveils a mission that captures one's imagination and commitment; it is something that totally absorbs a person and is of high interest.

People who are so deeply absorbed in a calling are said to have an autotelic personality. In discussing commitment, Mihalyi Csikszentmihalyi noted that *autotelic* is a word composed of two Greek roots: *auto* ("self") and *telos* ("goal"). An autotelic activity is one we do for its own sake because to experience it is to find a calling, which has its own rewards. "The autotelic experience, or flow, lifts the course of life to a different level. Alienation gives way to involvement, enjoyment replaces boredom, helplessness turns into a feeling of control, and psychic energy works to reinforce the sense of self, instead of being lost in the service of external goals. When experience is intrinsically rewarding life is justified in the present, instead of being held hostage to a hypothetical future gain."[7]

People with an autotelic self know that they have freely chosen whatever goal they are pursuing. A calling becomes self-absorbing and involving and is the ground in which life's purpose is nurtured and grown.

EDUCATION, VALUES, AND THE SOUL OF SCHOOLS

Students' imagination and enthusiasm to pursue ideas, knowledge, and passion are the intangible gifts that come from a quality education and relationship between teacher and student. The resulting motivation not only provides satisfaction to the individual but also produces creative and energizing ideas and solutions to society's problems and issues.

Places in which children learn should not be subject only to scientific management and engineering. Using corporate language to describe schools is bogus. Schools are not competitive businesses. Production-line jargon is inappropriate for schools, while the language of philosophy—soul, goodness, and virtue—is more proper for the education of children. The use of these philosophical words and ideas alters the mindscapes used for thinking about schools and what they should be.

Schools have a deep and important purpose. They have a sacred covenant to nourish, inspire, and love children—to teach them the cognitive, intellectual, and ethical responsibilities they need to find their place in the world and to help them find themselves, so the "real" person may surface.

The concept of soul concerns commitment and fulfillment and a moral and ethical imperative that goes beyond self-interest. Soul involves the high-mindedness of purpose, the warmth of feeling, the excitement of spirit and imagination, and the grace and courage that people demonstrate. It has to do with appreciation and joy for the gifts and potential of children intellectually, artistically, personally, and physically.

The soul of a school comprises the guiding principles that govern the school and the people who work in it. It is about heart, insight, wisdom, and what inspires people intellectually and philosophically. It creates an environment in which children and teachers are fulfilled as individual people. It crafts the nature of life within each classroom and in the hallways. It imparts a sense of goodness—a good school is a good place to teach and learn—which involves honor, virtue, and integrity.

Goodness as a concept seems old-fashioned and not a worthy subject of table talk at educational conferences or seminars. But there is beauty in the unpretentious lack of jargon surrounding "goodness": it is an intangible in a metrically driven world, and it requires moving beyond hollow, data-based patter and decisions based on ethics and principles and humanity.

Good schools treat people justly, with human decency, kindness, politeness, compassion, generosity, mercy, fairness, and respect. As a result of the goodness that comes from teachers, students are able to grow, fulfill their potential, and act in ways that enhance their community. There is "good" will toward others in the school, and "good" habits of the mind and body are taught and reinforced.

Ethics and values form the foundation of a school. Judgments and decisions are made that are centered on noble values and principles around which the school operates. Goodness and learning involve justice, truth, equality, beauty, integrity, excellence, and quality.

Acting with goodness also includes the concept of love—not romantic or familial love, but love nonetheless, especially when it comes to the children in the community. It is selfless love—agape—love that accepts, forgives, and believes in people's common good.

Bill O'Brien, former chief executive officer of Hanover Insurance, in his book, *Character at Work*, indicated that leaders must "love" the people with whom they work. He said, "We have to understand what love is. Love is not limited to romance, family, and friends, but extends to every human endeavor, including the conduct of commerce. By 'love' I mean a predisposition towards helping another person to become complete."[8]

In schools, industrial-corporate approaches and language distract us from the real mission of schools, which is really to provide sanctuaries based on goodness and ethics. The virtue of an education is that it liberates and elevates the mind and spirit. Schools are places where individuals find knowledge and wisdom but also discover themselves— seeing themselves clearly for the first time. Creativity is important in all facets of learning, from the academic to the artistic to the philosophical.

All of this leads to the issue of what students and citizens should be able to think about. What knowledge and exposure do they need to ideas that form their individual self and society?

BINARY THINKING

Thinking in a certain way—a mindset—can be a barrier to finding a sense of self-identity. Certainty is not always clear in real-life situations and problems. There are invisible forces, a lack of information, or even a clear definition of the issues that are in play. Life's circumstances are complex and can cloud certainty with regard to options and answers. Life is not always black and white.

In many schools, black-and-white thinking is predominant. Answers are either right or wrong. In many cases, students do not have to understand *why* they are right or wrong; instead, students just have to know which choice is right or wrong on a test.

However, right versus wrong is not always that clear: there are circumstances and principles that can fog the answer. The rightness or wrongness of an answer may be dependent on other factors: situations, values, or standards. Are there moral or physical circumstances where lying, for example, is not wrong? During grievous situations and totalitarian context, like the Holocaust, could lying be the right thing to do when another's life is at stake? Moral values can outweigh the virtue of telling the truth, whereas other circumstances may allow for a binary—right or wrong—means of response.

Binary thinking can keep individuals stuck in a black-and-white view of the world, which can lead to an unfair use of information to sustain one's case or position or lead to conflict or failure. Frequently, there are more than two options available, but a binary view of life eliminates other options or the possibility of compromise. Some social situations are complex and complicated, raising a multitude of options, residual results, and pressures. Standing silent on issues is a choice—a third one—that also is not free of ethical or moral implications and consequences.

In personal relationships or organizations of all types, binary thinking exists. In personal contacts, the phrase "It's my way or the highway" is an example: compromise or thoughtful reflection and the ability to develop other options don't exist. Discussion of alternatives is lost. But things are not always black or white. They're more complicated due to emotion, knowledge, experience, and personal needs. Human beings and their motivations are not always easy to evaluate because complexity and emotions are not always obvious or clear and can be open to multiple interpretations.

The fallacy of binary thinking is that only two options or choices exist. Creativity and compromise do not rely solely on binary thought. Limiting options to two choices in personal and human relations is not characteristic of critical and complex thinking. In addition, interpretations of circumstances are framed from individual perspectives and mindsets.

Critical thinking has been a goal of education. Many employers require employees who are critical and reflective thinkers. Actually, thinking ability and a quality liberal arts education are attractive to employers, because thinking across disciplines and insight into human motivation and emotion enhance the simple application of facts, ideas, and systems.

Howard Gardner, in his book *Five Minds for the Future*, classifies the different "minds" necessary in a complex and changing world. He asserts that ethics and meaning are vitally important in living a good life. The five minds are these:

- Disciplined mind—has mastered at least one way of thinking that characterizes a specific scholarly discipline, craft, or profession
- Synthesizing mind—takes pieces of information from disparate sources, understands and evaluates them objectively, and puts them together in ways that makes sense
- Creative mind—breaks new ground and presents ideas, raises questions, and asserts fresh ways of thinking
- Respectful mind—welcomes differences between groups and individuals and tries to understand and work with them
- Ethical mind—conceptualizes how people can serve purposes beyond self-interest and work unselfishly on principle[9]

In actuality, life requires the application of all of these "minds." All of them are needed to discover and gain insight into answering the question "Who am I?" Understanding self and relationships require all of the minds that Gardner identifies.

Individuals must be able to think in scholarly ways and synthesize ideas. Creativity and ethics are essential to understand abstractions and apply them to reality. Simple either/or responses may not be complex enough to analyze situations and determine thoughtful and unique answers.

In addition, questioning is important. Ways to frame questions range from soliciting simple knowledge and recall to the more complex ones that require analysis, synthesis, and evaluation. Responding to higher-order questions requires a depth of thinking and understanding. Being able to question intelligently requires knowledge and understanding.

PLUSES AND MINUSES

"Intelligence is morally neutral."[10] An individual's intelligence does not always predict his or her moral perspective or civility. History has examples of highly intelligent people following disastrous paths of questionable moral standing.

Most individuals, at one time or another, have questioned their behavior, attitude, or choices. Questioning produces insight about motives and approaches as well as the goodness of their decisions as individuals. Understanding the past, comprehending what principles support democracy and government, and protecting one's rights are absolutely essential in determining a moral and ethical course.

Today, technology is perceived as a positive and essential aspect of personal, professional, and social life. In fact, individuals cannot seem to live without it: not tapping into social media sites, tweets, or emails creates stress and anxiety. People generally view these activities positively, however, just accepting technological advances as virtuous, without the ability to assess the "dark" side of how they may be implemented. That failure to make balanced assessment is shortsighted and dangerous to the individual and democracy.

Technology is not evil, but it is also not blindly virtuous. Many tools can be used for either good or evil purposes. The same is true for technology. Each individual must shape his or her life and find meaning. Technology should not shape the direction of one's life. It is simply a tool that serves people, not vice versa. Products of technology, a tool, have no link to virtue or ethics; they are simply gadgets. False news, screen addiction, and loss of privacy are just some of the negatives of using and applying technology. In addition, privacy is threatened through technology, as the large corporations have demonstrated.

Brainpower does not guarantee moral and ethical action. In society, innovation has brought about means of communication, education, and connection that were unknown fifty years ago. Well-intentioned innovation always brings forth both positive and negative consequences. In addition, concerns must be addressed, particularly those unanticipated issues that raise questions of ethics, fairness, and moral principle. Significant change will mark the rest of the century and beyond, as has happened in the past hundred years.

An education that includes ethics and moral expectations, which are essential in fast-changing times, is necessary for individuals to gain moral clarity and wisdom. Discussing truth and understanding and working through the clash of two positive principles (i.e., privacy and security) are essential as new breakthroughs in science, technology, and biotechnology occur.

Information is more easily available than ever before. Pertinent questions about this information are: Is it accurate and reliable? and What should I do with it? Children today and tomorrow will have to make sense of what is true and objective and how it relates to them and the future. Ethics has become a basic subject all students must study. A complex world, coupled with mass technology, requires clarity of ethics and standards.

Perspective

Perspective . . .
one of those indefinable things.
Are any two exactly the same?
Do they change with age
or are they soldered in principle,
simply adrift with the times?
Is perspective related to truth?
Or, is it simply a belief,
coupled to opinions, or
the product of ignorance?
What gives birth to perspective?
The gestation of feelings or thought?
Other people standing on the platform
of knowledge, relationships, power?
Or, are they pinnacles of wisdom?
Are they irrelevant to the
growing independence of judgment
that slowly evolves with time?
Sometimes viewpoints are
driven by the darkness of minds,
locked in closets of arrogance,
fear, lost confidence or insecurity.
Other times, the soft whispers
of values and principles modify
former views and muddled thoughts
as the light of reason punctures

the fog of fallacy and deception,
and brings truth to light.

WHAT TO REMEMBER

- The purpose of education is more than employment: understanding principles, values, and ethics for a life filled with change is critically important.
- Mentors are critical in helping students become aware of their abilities in order to pursue their self-fulfilling aspirations.
- Students are not sheep—they must develop themselves as human beings to fulfill their potential and serve others and society.
- Ethics, principles, and values must be a part of educational discussions and content, which are invaluable in a fast-changing and innovative society.
- Intelligence and technology are morally neutral. Their application requires principled and ethical thinking.
- Risk-taking and failure are part of life and education. Fear of failure is detrimental to growth.
- Everyone's uniqueness and calling should be nurtured and be a part of an individual's self-understanding and self-concept.
- The soul of school concerns the acceptance, nurturing, and development of students to expand their talent, nourish their spirit, and promote their internal goodness.

NOTES

1. Buchanan, Ash, "The Purpose of Education: Becoming Yourself So You Can Contribute to Society," *Medium*, July 10, 2016.

2. Deresiewicz, William, *Excellent Sheep* (New York: Free Press, 2014), 21.

3. Deresiewicz, *Excellent Sheep*, 22.

4. Deresiewicz, *Excellent Sheep*, 84.

5. Deresiewicz, *Excellent Sheep*, 90.

6. The Center for Courage & Renewal, and Francis, Shelly L., *The Courage Way: Leading and Living with Integrity* (San Francisco: Berrett-Koehler Publishers, 2018), loc. 1660, Kindle.

7. Csikszentmihalyi, Mihaly, *Flow* (New York: Harper Perennial Modern Classic, HarperCollins, 2008), 69, Kindle.

8. O'Brien, Bill, *Character at Work* (New York: Paulist Press, 2008), 105.

9. Gardner, Howard, *Five Minds for the Future* (Boston: Harvard Business Press, 2009), 3.

10. Hedger, Chris, *Empire of Illusion* (New York: Nation Books, 2009), 104.

9

DEFINING MOMENTS

Our moments of inspiration are not lost though we have no particular poem to show for them; for those experiences have left an indelible impression, and we are ever and anon reminded of them.

—Henry David Thoreau

I believe we are solely responsible for our choices, and we have to accept the consequences of every deed, word, and thought throughout our lifetime.

—Elisabeth Kubler-Ross

Times and events in life become embossed in memory. They are significant and consequential because of their impact on one's self and perception. The impact, at first glance, can be subtle but then blossom into a lifelong point of view. Others are heart-stopping and alter life and outlook almost immediately. They may be singular occurrences or evolve collectively over a period of time. In any event they become threshold moments.

Poet John O'Donohue stated,

At any time you can ask yourself: At which threshold am I now standing? At this time in my life, what am I leaving? Where am I about to enter? What is preventing me from crossing my next threshold? What gift would enable me to do it? A threshold is not a simple boundary; it is a lovely testimony to the fullness and integrity of an experience or stage of life that it intensifies toward the end into a real frontier that cannot be crossed without the heart being passionately

engaged and woken up. At this threshold a great complexity of emotions comes alive: confusion, fear, excitement, sadness, hope. . . . It is
wise in your own life to be able to recognize and acknowledge the
key thresholds; to take your time; to feel all the varieties of presence
that accrue there; to listen inward with complete attention until you
hear the inner voice calling you forward. The time has come to
cross.[1]

O'Donohue uses the word *threshold*. While not totally synonymous,
defining moments are thresholds because they open the doorway to
change introspectively and to the greater world and relationships. At
times, one forges a new beginning in a different or clearer light. These
moments may come through conversations, relationships, experiences—serious, sad, or joyful—creating greater insight and self-awareness. A moment of introspection may awaken one and provide insight
into the depth of an experience or relationship.

Defining moments are times or events that open a new course and
deeper personal understanding or insight. They clarify and define individuals—who they are, that is, their essential nature and character.
These moments cannot always be planned: they occur without intention
and not necessarily when an individual's attention and presence are
ready.

"A defining moment is a point in your life when you're urged to
make a pivotal decision, or when you experience something that fundamentally changes you. Not only do these moments define us, but they
have a transformative effect on our perceptions and behaviors."[2] These
moments influence how individuals understand and perceive themselves, because they touch the heart and spirit or uncover a sense of
what is truly important to them in various aspects of their lives. They
provide an unexpected external view of their attitude, behavior, thinking, or influence.

What is consequential and meaningful can get buried in trying to
please others, to meet others' desires, or to follow paths that are
contrary to their own yearning, passion, or ideals—all of which can be
debilitating to one's heart and soul.

Defining moments arise in all stages of life and in all circumstances.
They open a threshold to a clearer perspective of self and presence and
enlarge the pathway ahead by raising decisions of what to do and in
what direction. Being true to oneself and what success and failure are,

become clearer. Principles, values, and ethics present options and direction. The determination to act on these moments may be subtle through self-understanding or through direct and specific actions or perspectives. These decisions require thought and self-reflection.

MINDSCAPES AND PERSPECTIVE

An individual's mindscape develops early in childhood and directs the view of the world and of life. Home, school, playgrounds, neighborhoods, and communities provide experiences that create feelings and plant memories. People and relationships heavily influence the perspectives of children as they grow into maturity.

In reality, "adults carry the memory, expectations, and emotions of their own experiences as school children. . . . As long as our thinking is governed by habit—notably by industrial, 'machine age' concepts such as control, predictability, standardization, and 'faster is better'—we will continue to re-create institutions as they had been formed."[3] Understanding the world and relationships comes from experiences. Mindscapes are built around these encounters and insights.

Perspective is created by thoughts, values, and experiences: what is seen and how it is interpreted. Two people observing and experiencing the same event may have very different interpretations. In many ways, people's respective mindsets direct their responses, because through mindset, they perceive and interpret the world around them.

Individuals must consider how they think and how their mind works. Being aware of one's own thoughts is important for grasping how the self responds to situations; at times, fear arises or feelings of awkwardness or incompetence surface, causing people to back away from circumstances.

Learning about oneself is essential for understanding what needs are rising and what is happening in the greater context. Many times, individuals do not always perceive or understand how words, attitudes, and actions affect others and events. To understand situations, one must have a sense of what has happened and what is emerging, which requires not only cognitive understanding but also a sense of emotional, philosophical, and moral comprehension of situations and opportunities.

DEFINING MOMENTS

Defining moments do not announce themselves with a bugle fanfare or a cymbal crash. In many cases, only in retrospect and contemplation does one realize the impact of a moment. Sometimes, if individuals are "present"—fully conscious, aware of the current moment and of their preconceptions[4]—they are of aware of the significant defining moment taking place. At other times, only in looking back will they appreciate the event or experience. Quiet awareness, presence, and listening are important for recognizing defining moments.

Several types of defining moments occur: some concern loss or achievement, right versus wrong conflict, or right versus right situations.

Loss

> Curtis was sitting at his desk working on a writing project. He was thinking back to a time more than sixty years ago, when he was four years old. He remembered sitting under the dining room table with his sister, Betty, who was four years older. He recalled a conversation he had with her years ago, when he asked her, "Do you remember the night Dad died?"
>
> "Yes; I'll never forget that day!" she said. "I remember the police car's red lights flashing on the walls and . . . and the firemen's boots. I'll never forget them—seeing them by looking out from under the table. Remember? . . . We both sat there together."
>
> "Yeah, under the dining room table! The boots! Me too. It's funny that you and I remember the boots from that night." He paused and said softly, "I wonder how my life would have been different if Dad had lived. Would I have been as shy in grade school and so unsure of myself? How would Dad have affected my attitudes, relationships, and interests? Would I be who I am today, or would I be someone entirely different?"
>
> Betty looked at him. "I was older than you and I have a few more memories of him. But I wonder about that too. . . . We'll never know."

A defining moment! The death of a parent. Two kids wondering how they might be different if a father had lived. They both wanted more detailed knowledge of who he was as a person—his character, his values, or even the sound of his voice. How would they have traversed the issues they faced growing up and even now if he had lived? The memory of the loss survives into older age: the experience was defining because of absence—of a parent's love, character, and wisdom on the children's move through childhood and into maturity.

Certainly loss is a powerful defining moment, caused by what happened, what might have been, and, in this case, the psychological and emotional impact that occurs at the death of a parent at a young age. Even in his late sixties, Curtis still looks back and can feel the gravity of the situation and how his life's path might have been influenced if his father had lived. In retrospect, that event weighs heavier on him now in some respects than when he was in the fast-moving, goal-focused days of young adulthood. A big issue was that he never had a father to model fatherhood for him with his own children.

Survivors of such a loss contend with what has been called "paradoxically, the absent memory." Maxine Harris in her book, *The Loss That Is Forever*, discusses a case similar to Curtis and Betty's:

> One man whose father died when he was three said, "There is a hole there when I think of my father. It is marked by absence, not just for my own father, but for the role of father as well. I don't know what 'father' means. When I started school, I remember feeling different from other kids who had a mother and a father. All I had was a mother. I had no father; that was my life. I didn't know anything else. I didn't know anything about a father. It's not like a reverse image or even a shadow. There was no image, just me, my brother, and my mother; that was my family." When he moved beyond the orbit of his immediate family, he encountered other children, other families, and knew that something was missing in his own life. Father became that which was absent, and his ideas about his own father and a more general image of "father" were built up around this absent image.[5]

In this circumstance, fate—not choice—created the defining moment that altered lives dramatically and forever. Possible future relationships and opportunities were irreversibly altered through loss by the absence of a fatherly experience. It causes people, at times, to wonder, "Why me?" and "Who would I have been?"

Right versus Wrong

Julia sat in her office perplexed. Her boss, Emerson, sent her a message to come to her office ASAP. She wondered, "What can that be about?" She walked over to Emerson's office and the executive assistant said to her, "Go right on in. She's waiting for you."

"Glad you're here, Julia. Let's sit down at the conference table," Emerson said. "Would you like any coffee or tea? Help yourself." She pulled out a file folder and grabbed Julia's report. "I read your report for the board's next meeting. Overall, it is well done."

"I know the importance of this issue for you and the board, and I understand it has implications for the new program you are going to recommend," Julia commented.

"Yes, yes it does. That's why I need to talk with you. Board members consider you in high regard. You have credibility based on your past performance."

"I have worked very hard to garner their respect—and yours."

"I know, and I appreciate your work. I have plans for a position of more authority for you in the very near future. A high-level management position will be opening soon."

"Thank you. I really enjoy working with you and with everybody in the office," Julia replied.

"Here's the thing, Julia. Your third conclusion in the summary puts the top management and me in a less-than-desirable position and light. It also raises questions about the new program that we worked very hard to resolve. What you wrote raises a series of potential issues. I would like you to reconsider and eliminate that conclusion."

Julia hesitated. "But . . . but the research, interviews, data, and many staff vigorously support that conclusion. Taking it out would not be giving the board the total analysis. Ethically it. . . . If I take it out, it weakens the thoroughness of the entire report in my opinion. My reputation and integrity would be damaged with colleagues and eventually with the board."

"Julia," Emerson said, sliding the report across the conference table toward her. "Take another look at this report in light of our conversation and meet me here at 1:30 today and let me know."

Julia faces a difficult issue: Does she live up to her professional standards of credibility and integrity, or does she compromise the report and alter its accuracy and truthfulness to please her boss? If she changes the report, will she pass the "sleep test"? Will she be able to sleep at night if she isn't true to herself and her standards for her work?

Are pleasing the boss and the allure of a promotion and maintaining Emerson's confidence and respect for her going to take precedence? This could be a pivotal decision for Julia: either to stand on principle and risk the boss's ire or to ensure her future professionally and financially in the company and make the change.

The situation has the potential to affect transitions in her career. Decisions such as these are true matters of character. They challenge integrity and honesty and issues of loyalty and commitment. While not life or death, they do reflect the internal character of a person; is the person one who will compromise professional standards for the prospect of personal gain and to maintain the confidence of her superiors, or stand by the report and meet her own professional standards and integrity? Professional perspectives and individual principles can collide in these situations. If Julia compromises the report, she may lose the respect of her superior; if she doesn't, she may lose it if this conversation was a test of her ethics.

Right versus Right

Luke leaned back in his chair and ran his hands through his hair. He thought, "What an issue! What are you supposed to do?" He was perplexed. There are at least two ways to address the situation: What is the best answer?

In a confidential meeting, Luke's boss discussed with him and three other colleagues the five-year enrollments and projections. His boss indicated, "We will have to reduce staff at the central office and several schools. The fiscal numbers just don't work out. Cuts will have to be made. Obviously, you have to keep this confidential. Some legal questions have to be cleared up, plus, at some point, I am going to have to meet with board members in an executive session. And, of course, the unions will have to be brought in when the time is right. Right now, we can't have any leaks."

As a top central-office administrator, Luke has to maintain confidentiality. If he did not, he would violate his responsibility to his boss and lose his trust. In addition, it would diminish the ability to resolve a serious program and financial issue that affects opportunities for children and the staffing necessary to keep them operational.

Three days later, Luke's good friend Callan, an administrator of a supplementary program who works with him in the central office, came up to him and said quietly, "Can I speak with you confidentially?"

"Sure," he replied. They walked to a small conference room and closed the door.

"Luke, there's a rumbling in the office that there may be layoffs. Is that true?"

Luke looked at him and hesitated. "When did you hear that?"

"Yesterday," Callan paused. "Listen Luke, I don't have much seniority here. You've been great in helping me get this job. As you know, I have to work. . . . I have kids in elementary school . . . one with special needs. You recruited me and I came here because of you and the priorities you identified. If there's a possibility I may lose my job, I need to know. I will have to start looking. I've always considered you my friend, even though you're my boss."

Luke's ethical dilemma is this: As part of his professional role, keeping things confidential is a major responsibility and ethical requirement. But as a colleague as well as a friend, being truthful and honest is a basic expectation in order to maintain trust and credibility. A needy friend, who is going through a dramatic change, has asked Luke for guidance that could impact the friend's family's needs and financial security. Should Luke live up to his professional standards and obligations or live up to his personal values and standards as a friend? Should he tell the truth or not?

Decisions have consequences. The impact on others in the organization is an important issue. In right-versus-right circumstances, which course of action will do the most good and least harm? What will be the best for the most? What has the most moral and ethical value? Professionally, Luke has duties and obligations. Personally, he faces his professional responsibilities and ethics, and he must confront his conscience and values as a friend to a person who has family obligations.

Joseph Badaracco wrote the definitive book *Defining Moments*, about the dilemmas of decisions in business as well as in personal life. He indicated that these moments bring to focus "who am I? and what do I stand for?"[6] These issues define a person's character as well as define the person to others, which is a major concern and issue in each of these moments.

An individual in these circumstances may consider what "feelings and intuitions are coming into conflict in the situation."[7] People's feelings in these situations help them make sense of the issue, understand basic concerns, and determine the stakes at play. Feelings and intuitions "are both a form of intelligence and a source of insight." This makes the circumstances, whether at work or in private life, personal.

A second consideration is: Which of the responsibilities and values that are in conflict are deeply rooted in my life and the communities I care about? Responding to this question should reflect what principles and commitments are most consequential and clarify what actions would be most in harmony with them.

Individuals confront right-versus-right dilemmas at work, in the community, and in their personal life. In all, there may be competing priorities and interpretations of the issue. These moments can cause individuals to find a balance between their heart and its "idealism" and the pragmatic role they play in the reality of the workplace or elsewhere.

Four questions can help assess how to resolve right-versus-right dilemmas.[8] First, which course of action will do the most good and the least harm? Second, which alternative serves others' rights? Third, what plan is consistent with basic values and commitments? Fourth, which course of action is feasible in the world as it is?

These four questions involve consequences, the greatest good for the greatest number; rights, the question of what rights are at play; conscience of values, the impact of the decision on one's character; and pragmatism, whether a particular solution will work.

Right-versus-right moments define the values that are of the highest priority. In addition, they "may surface something hidden. They can crystallize what was fluid and unformed. They may give a sharp, clear view of something previously obscure. In every case, however, a defining moment reveals something important about a person's basic values and about his or her abiding commitments in life."[9]

The examples of Curtis, Julia, and Luke raise important issues about the direction these individuals will take. Questions of values arise, along with the possible conflict of wants, desires, and needs. Julia and Luke face situations that confront two aspects of their lives: personal and professional. These situations concern both and include other people's perspective of and respect for them. Sacrificing professional or personal regard is not easy. In both cases, relationships are at stake.

Some defining moments are of smaller, yet powerful, magnitude and are provided frequently by the decisions of others on the basis of care and friendship.

Jack hustled to the office of his major advisor in college. He was completing his junior year and making plans for his senior classes with his advisor, Dr. Meyer, who is a bit formal about being on time.

"Jack, good to see you. You got here on time! Thank you!"

"It's been a crazy day, Dr. Meyer. Whattaya mean 'on time'? I'm always on time, eh," he chuckled. Jack sat down in a chair next to Dr. Meyer's desk.

"Jack, I want to talk to you, because I have a great deal of respect for you and your talent. You're doing a great job in your classes—you also provide a different perspective to our class discussions because of your urban background. Your papers are well done and thoughtful."

"Thanks. My high school teachers would never believe I'm in college and gettin' a degree in history. I have to thank you for your help."

"You've done well—should be proud. But I have to talk to you about one thing that can get in your way. And I tell you this because I care about you, your ability, and your future possibilities and career."

"Yes," Jack said, wondering where this conversation was going.

"Jack, it's your diction. You sometimes talk with a Chicago accent. 'Whatta' for 'what do,' 'dose' for 'those,' 'you know' at the end of sentences." Dr. Meyer leaned forward in his chair toward Jack.

Jack froze in his seat and listened. He saw and felt the quiet concern of Dr. Meyer, who supported him in so many ways, including the special programs and employment.

"I tell you this, Jack, because you have so much talent that I don't want something like that to get in your way. I really appreciate having you as an advisee, and I say this because I don't want something like this—diction—to deflect people from your ability. You have a bright future."

The conversation with Dr. Meyer stayed with Jack throughout his life. He became aware of his formal diction and went on to many leadership positions. Even in his later years he talked to friends and students about that defining moment in conversation. Jack's wife said a number of times, "I can tell when Jack is on a business call on the phone; his voice changes and he becomes more formal and distinct."

Self-awareness is a part of these interactions and situations. Individuals who reflect on their own standards and beliefs are more likely to try to maintain integrity to them. In addition, they are likely to take responsibility for their decisions and actions. All defining moments bring self-reflection and inquiry. Understanding who you *are* often requires understanding who you *were*.

Defining moments shape a person. In Curtis's case, the death of a father shaped him differently than had he not faced this intense and lifelong loss. It was a major factor in forming his character. Childhood perspectives, thoughts, and feelings in such a difficult circumstance, and the void it created, framed his character. Feeling different, questioning why, and confronting intense grief can move people in diverse ways and directions.

In addition, individuals have unexpected situations and interactions that are minor at the time but have significant long-term impact, opening or closing some doors forever. Meeting people and confronting circumstances can affect individuals deeply; both can provide needed help and perspective. "Two or more events" can coincide to produce synchronicity (as discussed earlier). [10]

In facing life and its consequences, not only experiences but also other people are essential. As stated earlier, there are polestars. They are not just people who provide information or verbal support. They go further. Their concern is for the well-being of their subjects, whom they provide not only with support but also with direct, but caring, feedback about what may be getting in the way in relating to others or communicating. Caring includes presenting, in a compassionate and kindhearted manner, difficult things that are necessary for subjects to hear in order to grow.

Life is dynamic, with subtle as well as obvious forces at work within each person along with the impact of external relationships and society. How people perceive experiences varies. Experiences form attitudes and opinions. In addition, ideas and perceptions are very powerful because they influence both the mind and the soul.

The formation of individuals is an ongoing process. As Nietzsche stated, "The creation of self is not a static episode, a final goal which, once obtained, forecloses the possibility of continuing to change and develop."[11]

CHARACTER

"Humility and honesty, along with courage, are important in addressing challenges and defeat. Quiet reflection is a significant tool to understand how and why events happened as they did. Sometimes pure reason is not sufficient. Self-understanding is powerful in finding a new way to address situations and the fortitude to move ahead. In a real sense, character, not personality or self-esteem, defines a person's destiny."[12]

In any circumstance of life—ethical, moral, personal, social, political, or other—a person's character is what matters and what others remember. Character and credibility are pivotal points others use to determine whether a relationship will develop, continue, or fade.

Character is built, in part, by those defining moments people experience from childhood through adulthood. Those moments create a sense of inner wisdom that "informs our lives and leadership. It is our identity and integrity, the sum of our shadows and light, our true self."[13]

In finding a sense of self, people confront several things. One is self-doubt, which affects both children and adults. This doubt can stymie a person's motivation, particularly when values and ethics are at risk.

A sense of character is important in extinguishing the fear of losing and being defeated. Standing up takes character and fortitude, but standing in the shadows away from scrutiny may also compromise one's inner sense of self. History has serious examples of individuals and groups standing silent while moral breakdowns occur in public.

Self-understanding provides the inner knowledge and the courage to pursue one's values and meaning. Integrity and credibility create a sense of self-understanding and wholeness that helps answer the question, Who am I? "Self-awareness starts with understanding that self is more than your outer image, your job title, your identity in relation to others (mother, father, sister, brother, friend, spouse, colleague). True self is fundamentally good, even with its shadows, because it is already whole. True self is your hidden wholeness—it's not always in plain sight but it's there."[14]

Individuals determine their attitude and response. To do so requires finding one's voice, making hard choices, and choosing a direction in harmony with values, beliefs, and ethics—being true to oneself.

Moral courage is necessary. As Rushworth Kidder wrote, "In the defining moments of our lives . . . values count for little without the willingness to put them into practice. Without moral courage, our brightest virtues rust from lack of use. With it, we build piece by piece a more ethical world." [15]

Today, as in the past, individuals need the moral courage to act with character and do what is right. Action on those defining moments that lit their internal light, self-understanding, and moral responsibility is necessary to create a good society and life.

Cousins

Does fierce independence
give way to isolation?
Two cousins living in
the same stream of thought.
Both born of different mothers
One from courage and optimism
To face the future in
Unwavering faith in possibility.
The other born of fear
Abandonment taught by mortality and death
Or from rational reflection and evaporation
Of love and care.
Two cousins with similar genes
But vitally different in texture
One born with certainty and power
The other fertilized by loss and anxious waiting.
Independence lives in the light of confidence
Isolation swelters in the shadow of doubt
The difference cannot be seen by those outside
Only by those who look in the mirror's reflection.

WHAT TO REMEMBER

- Defining moments clarify and define who individuals are: their character and nature. These are pivotal points in clarifying a sense of self, and they occur in all stages of life.
- The mindscapes of individuals are developed from their experiences and relationships, which live in their memories and formulate their perspectives of current experiences.
- Defining moments occur through loss or achievement, right-versus-wrong conflict, or the confrontation of right-versus-right dilemmas.
- Defining moments shape a person and have a long-term impact in all facets of his or her life.
- A person's character and management of situations—personal, professional, or social—matter and are built, in part, through defining moments.
- Self-understanding provides the internal knowledge and courage to live with integrity and credibility to ethical standards.

NOTES

1. O'Donohue, John, *To Bless the Space between Us* (New York: Doubleday, 2008), 48–49.

2. Evans, Sydney, "How to Define Your Defining Moments," *Forbes*, August 3, 2017, https://www.forbes.com/sites/forbescoachescouncil/2017/08/03/how-to-define-your-defining-moments/#4608aea725d0.

3. Senge, Peter M., et al., *Presence: An Exploration of Profound Change in People, Organizations, and Society* (New York: Crown Publishing Group, 2005), loc. 177, Kindle.

4. Senge et al., *Presence*, loc. 247.

5. Harris, Maxine, *The Loss That Is Forever* (New York: Penguin Group, 1995), 18.

6. Badaracco, Joseph L., Jr., *Defining Moments: When Managers Must Choose between Right and Right* (Boston: Harvard Business Review Press, 2016), 18, Kindle.

7. Badaracco, Joseph L., Jr., "The Discipline of Building Character," *Harvard Business Review* (March/April 1998): 4–5.

8. Christiansen, David S., and Boneck, Robin, "Four Questions for Analyzing the Right-versus-Right Dilemmas of Managers," *Journal of Basic Case Studies* 6, no. 3 (May/June 2010): 54–55.

9. Badaracco, *Defining Moments*, 57.

10. Jaworski, Joseph, *Synchronicity* (San Francisco: Berrett-Koehler Publishers, 1996), 88.

11. Badaracco, *Defining Moments*, 94.

12. Goens, George A., *It's Not My Fault: Victim Mentality and Becoming Response-able.* (Lanham, MD: Rowman & Littlefield, 2017), 51, Kindle.

13. Center for Courage & Renewal, and Francis, Shelly L., *The Courage Way: Leading and Living with Integrity* (San Francisco: Berrett-Koehler Publishers, 2018), loc. 974, Kindle.

14. Center for Courage & Renewal and Francis, *Courage Way*, loc. 1086.

15. Kidder, Rushworth M., *Moral Courage* (New York: HarperCollins, 2005), 3.

10

BIG QUESTIONS AND GREAT IDEAS

This above all; to thine own self be true.

—Shakespeare

At such a time it seems natural and good to me to ask myself these questions. What do I believe in? What must I fight for and what must I fight against?

—John Steinbeck

Conflict exists between the inner self and the ego. What one's ego wants is not an authentic reflection of a person's real self. Many times, the ego plants a false self—a façade of confidence, strength, and competence—when one's head barks anxiety, fear, and uncertainty. The self, however, speaks to what one loves and uplifts the spirit, the things that stir the soul and imagination.

Today, society places great pressure to conform to others' expectations and desires. Being popular is a major focus of technology—"Look at me! See what I am doing? Here I am!" Much is geared to getting approval and popularity. Most people are really devoid of any self-reflection or true identity: each "real" person is hidden behind a fabricated image, behind a screen, manipulated by algorithms and external recognition. Adolescents as well as adults of all ages can succumb to extraneous expectations and popularity. Status and social acceptance may divert one from finding a sense of self and self-identity.

Self has to do with who one is as a unique human being in essence, beliefs, and principles—basically what one stands for. Many people play it safe and simply report their "doings"—what they do for a living, what they generate, or what they accomplish—not who they are. People do things at work, in the community, and everywhere else. Doings are simplistic caricatures of people, constituting small slices of who people are and not anywhere close to a complete definition.

Ken Wilber contrasts doing values with being values. He states, "Making something, achieving something; they are often aggressive, competitive, and hierarchical; they are oriented toward the future; and they depend upon rules and judgment. . . . Being values, on the other hand, are values of increasing the present; values of accepting a person for what they are, not for what they can do; values of relationship, inclusion, acceptance, compassion, and care."[1]

Authenticity is a quality of being, while doing does not always embrace it. Being involves presence and awareness of experience, focusing on the moment. It involves living with integrity to oneself and building relationships with others. Showing one's true identity to others is sharing one's essence and core. One's being is housed in one's spirit and distinctive nature, character, and values.

As Parker Palmer stated, "Before I can tell my life what I want to do with it, I must listen to my life telling me who I am. I must listen for the truths and the values at the heart of my own identity, not the standards by which I *must* live—but the standards by which I cannot help but live if I am living my own life."[2]

Without a sense of self, individuals can get lost in a society pressing for compliance, celebrating diversion, and neglecting self-responsibility. Without understanding "self," people cannot live their values and principles, which are the cornerstones of personal integrity and honesty.

Individuals must understand it is more important to be themselves, living up to their values and commitments, than to be popular and simply go with the crowd. Being in vogue socially or politically may not be the right thing to do. Living up to the acceptance of others can damage character and stifle thinking anew about oneself and the future.

GOALS AND PRESENCE

According to Csikszentmihalyi, "The self can be considered a hierarchy of goals, because the goals define what we pay attention to, and how. If you know what goal takes precedence for a given person, you can generally anticipate where that person will invest psychic energy, and therefore predict his or her behavior."[3]

Many goals are similar for everyone: to be accepted, loved, respected, and to be secure and at ease. Once these basic goals are reasonably satisfied, individuals move to the self-development of their potential and aspirations. Self-actualization becomes a greater priority and integrates personal goals with larger ones of family, community, and purpose.

Peter Senge and his coauthors indicate that much behavior is based on habitual ways of learning and acting. They define it as "reactive learning . . . governed by 'downloading' habitual ways of thinking, of continuing to see the world within the familiar categories" with which individuals are comfortable.[4] Reactive learning is based on established mental models and habits—mindsets, as discussed earlier.

The self, however, is faced with an evolving whole—environment, society, and world—with which it must contend. Senge and his coauthors believe that, in facing life and its choices, a necessary core capacity is "presence,"[5] which means being "fully conscious and aware in the present moment" and engaging in "deep listening, of being open beyond one's preconceptions and historical ways of making sense." Letting go of all identities, conceptions, and stereotypes is necessary to respond to emerging change from science, the creative arts, and one's own experiences and relationships.

"Presencing," according to Otto Scharmer and Katrin Kaufer, "is a blended word combining sensing (feeling the future possibility) and presence (the state of being in the present moment). It means sensing and actualizing one's highest future possibility—acting from the presence of what is wanting to emerge."[6] In life, things are always unfolding, and people must move out of old ways of thinking and shift perception to what is evolving.

In presencing and looking inward, several principles are at play. First, individuals must shift attention from what they want to avoid to what they want to bring into reality. Energy to make things happen follows attention. Stagnation and huddling in defensive postures are the antithesis to finding creative and relevant opportunities.

Observation is also important: stopping, reflecting, and allowing inner conceptions and knowledge to surface. Suspend old habits of thought and "with an open heart, we can empathize, or see a situation with the eyes of someone else. With an open will, we can let go and let the new come."

Presencing allows new perspectives and ideas to come forth and for anxiety and obstacles of the past to be let go. In this process, the voice of judgment, which can shut down an open mind; cynicism, which can close an open heart; and fear, which deters an open will, must be curtailed.

Presencing helps people let go of the old and allows new ideas and perspectives to surface. Old patterns can be suspended and new ideas made to arise by seeing with fresh eyes. Answers to "Who am I?" and "Why am I here?" may emerge more clearly through silent reflection, introspection, and viewing life through a different lens. New perspectives can bring change not only in business and enterprise but also in one's life. Transformations happen as people perceive and think differently about the present state and what they want to emerge in the future.

KNOW THYSELF, AND SELF-REFLECTION

The phrase "Know thyself" goes back to ancient Greece but is just as pertinent today. In other words, individuals must know who they really are and what they are living for. Socrates proclaimed that an "unexamined life is not worth living." He was also concerned with the breakdown of human relations and how ignorance of doing the right thing could result in unethical behavior.

Moments of thoughtful reflection, however, do not always come easily. Many people have a difficult time when they look at themselves in the mirror and reflect on their relationships with others, how they think, what they think, and why they behave the way they do. Quiet contemplation and a moral conscience raise questions of self and conduct. It is much easier to speculate about other people and their thoughts and actions than it is to sit and self-evaluate.

Self-reflection is important to integrity and credibility. Engaging in self-denial and deflection is much easier than to look inward. Some individuals take on a victim mentality, blaming others or circumstances for their issues. They reject any semblance of self-responsibility for their own decisions, actions, or outcomes. The easy way out is to reject any personal responsibility. Victimhood is easier. Victimhood, however, is not a positive emotion about life and resilience and deflects any semblance of personal accountability.

Introspection requires conscious effort. People prefer to see themselves as they want to be seen by others. Self-reflection, however, raises uncomfortable matters of self-awareness, self-acceptance, and satisfaction with one's life. Some individuals always find excuses for their behavior, and then there are those who find fault in everything they do: they are hypercritical. Seeing oneself objectively is not always easy, but it is necessary.

Knowing thyself includes understanding one's strengths and weaknesses and knowledge and abilities. An examined life is important to a meaningful life because of the necessity to be resilient and face hardship and difficulty in an ethical and moral manner. Classifying and understanding one's choices and influences create insight and commitment to the road a person pursues.

Irving Singer defined the paths to a meaningful existence: "The cultivation of creativity itself, aesthetic contemplation, the pursuit of spiritual or humanitarian ideals, the full employment of one's energies, the realization of individual talents, the search for truth, the experiences of love in one or another of its modalities."[7]

John Dewey proposed that "human beings connect with the world via meanings; they do not just undergo 'events.' Perception, the act of discerning meaning, also leads to awareness, the act of seeking to understand meaning."[8] People search for meaning, and they desire to engage in the events that they perceive in that exploration.

Meaning, self-reflection, and understanding are interrelated because of the connection between people's actions and their beliefs. Education is, in part, defining beliefs and attitudes through comprehending values, principles, and ethics. From these and other experiences comes the development of a personal identity.

A sense of self drives motivation; goals reflect people's identity: who they are and what they stand for. Goals determine how individuals react to situations and other people and affect their demeanor and openness to ideas and discussion. Attitudes affect future effort and relationships and can be more important than reciting academic content.

An open mind in weighing questions tests one's beliefs. New evidence and different times issues may question one's personal perspectives and initiate changing one's mindset. In fact, challenging one's mind is a sign of character, because it takes strength to alter one's thinking and impressions. Questioning strongly held ideas or beliefs is not easy, because they are hard-baked into one's thinking through the influence of parents, experience, education, religion, and society. Ideas and concepts may be viewed differently as one's perspective is challenged.

Individuals' concept of virtue and the "good life" is a part of their self-definition and approach to life. Virtue involves being willing to consider things and contributions beyond self-interest, and treating others with respect and dignity in interactions and deeper relationships. It is the basis for integrity and relationships with oneself and others.

Good character is based on ethics and morality. Ethics are basic in the formation of good character and are the foundation for how individuals treat each other. They are the guiding standards for living a principled life. Ethical conduct is essential in all aspects of life: personal, social, and professional. Goodness presumes moral conduct in deference to principles and not necessarily to physical or personal self-interest.

Without examining and understanding principles, standards, and ethics, college students can "grow up as ethical illiterates and moral idiots, unprepared to cope with ordinary life experiences,"[9] according to Norman Lamm, former president of Yeshiva University. He believed that universities had a responsibility to offer moral guidance on the "nature of the good life, truth and goodness and beauty and the value of thought and reflection." Understanding great ideas and principles provides the basis for reflection and consideration of personal, as well as societal tenor or behavior.

Ethics are critically important in every facet of life because they direct the proper course for decisions. In society and personal affairs, moral imperatives become evident, and the issue of determining what is right and wrong is raised. Without ethics, actions would be self-indulgent and aimless.

Ethics provide a framework for reviewing and considering decisions and actions concerning goals, processes, and outcomes. An ethical course is trustworthy and acceptable. All major professions—medicine, law, education, and others—have codes of ethics, in which people's health and welfare are primary and professional decisions require that practitioners not only be knowledgeable but also have an ethical foundation.

Ethics "are the norms that a community defines and institutionalizes to prevent individuals from pursuing self-interest at the expense of others."[10] They define moral principles that govern behavior through moral values, and determine what is good, just, and correct in judgments. Ethics raise uncomfortable questions regarding goals and methods.

Ethics define who we are as individuals and as members of a society and a culture, because they govern thought and thought processes to find solutions. Character is not about fame; "it involves ethical conduct, integrity to principles and values, and courage to act on them even in the face of opposition."[11]

People take for granted that they will be treated respectfully, truthfully, and civilly. Behaving and doing the right thing equate to demonstrating virtue. Individuals without compassion or integrity do not act with honor. Character requires the courage to act on principle and ethics in all situations, whether right counters right, right counters wrong, or change includes loss or growth. All of the circumstances require a moral imperative and understanding.

STANDING ON PRINCIPLE

Examples exist of people who say one thing and then do another. They don't stand on principle. Politics seems to be overrun with that behavior. Hence, questions of trust, honesty, and character arise, and respect is tarnished or lost.

Standing on principle requires examining one's conscience. Was a decision or behavior based on principle, or was it based on personal gain, popularity, or the desires of others? Questions about the self-interest and the benefit of others are raised, along with questions of fortitude. Standing against the grain takes courage, because the reactions of others may be harsh.

Are there any "buts" concerning principle? Are there times when "it depends"? Can a principle be superseded by time, situations, or general will? Should one violate a positive principle even to achieve a "good" end? In addition, when several positive principles may be in play and may be in conflict, which one, if any, should take precedence?

History offers examples of positive principles being voided for a "good" or moral end: Should violence or nonviolent aggression be applied to deter a person or movement that is determined to do something considered immoral? Should free speech be restricted because some people are offended or fear violence? Is it plausible to do a wrong in order to resolve a wrong? Should one lie to defeat a questionable or unethical position?

The demands of life can be intense. People lose their way because of the profound pressure and conflicting demands placed on them. Stress with regard to time can obscure clarity when there is a demand for one to decide quickly or without all needed information or options.

Unless individuals have a clear sense of who they are and what principles and values they hold, they can and do go askew. Then they regret, in retrospect, the decisions or actions they made, and they wish they behaved otherwise.

Being true to oneself is not always an easy road; it requires self-examination and self-reflection. A lack of introspection can glue individuals in place without the ability to change; the result is a mindless existence. Comparing oneself to one's values is necessary in order to move through life and confront the vagaries of change.

TRUTH AND IDEAS

A major aspect of character rests on truth and the pursuit of truth. Truth and the search for truth raise questions. A major question today, as in the past, is basic: What is truth? This question prompts others: Is there more than one definition of truth? Is there really something called one's "own truth," or is it just a belief? Are differences of opinion matters of what is and what is not true? Is truth subjective or objective?

According to philosopher Mortimer Adler, "We speak truthfully when our speech corresponds or conforms to what we think. And there is truth in communication between persons when, in using words, their two minds correspond with one another. The ideas in one person's mind correspond to the ideas in the other."[12] Adler also states that truth is a property of statements or propositions—for example, two plus two equals four. He defines truth as the agreement of the mind with reality.[13] True ideas are those that can be validated and verified.

Liars deliberately deceive others by saying one thing while believing another. In education, the search for truth involves scholarly presentations and expertise. Over time, through research and experience, what was once perceived as the truth is proven to be otherwise (e.g., the earth is flat). Some would call such misperceptions "errors in knowledge," not outward lies, because no one knew any better with the information at hand.

Then there is opinion, which in society is pervasive. Some individuals know they do not know and are simply ignorant of the truth. Some who are in error suppose they know but do not know they do not know.[14] Consequently an opinion may be true or false. These discussions and explanations should be a part of education.

Being educated is a journey in search of truth, both externally in the greater world and internally in greater self-understanding. Indoctrination and education are two separate ventures. Indoctrination is to cast minds into a mold to follow a certain thought for others' aims and purposes. Education, on the other hand, is to move people on a course of continuous exploration and creativity.

A direct link exists between truth and happiness. To be happy is to be true to oneself, which means individuals know what really matters to them, what they really care about, and what principles they follow. It may be playing music or serving others or running a business or any other deep passion that has the intensity to drive and direct one's life.

Individuals can tell what matters because without it they are at a loss and no longer in their element. They are happy when they live authentically and follow their true calling. A calling is not the same for everyone. All individuals really have to find out what matters deeply to them. If they don't, they will drift about on a wave of confusion and indecision, trying to live someone else's life or being influenced by what others want done for the sake of their own happiness.

Caring about truth in personal and professional life requires several things:

- Open-mindedness—listen and hear both sides of an argument; knowledge is not always absolute and unchanging.

- Tolerance of others' opinions—yes, it's fun to engage in debate, but do it after listening respectfully without ridicule or epithets.
- Curiosity and attention to evidence—avoid pursuing courses that can be disastrous; question assumptions; explore reasons and motives.
- Awareness—keep your eyes open and see the world and what is happening.
- Intellectual courage—stand up for the truth, even if it hurts; be true to yourself.
- Ethics—never use fear or power to control others.

Doctrine or dogma can be blinding and binding. Belief can guide a search for truth, but it may not be the truth. Beliefs may be quite different from the facts.

In addition to truth, education must also explore the great ideas of justice, liberty, beauty, equality, and goodness. All of these are recognized as important concepts in American society. These ideas, plus truth, are ubiquitous throughout life, and they formulate our perceptions of self and society.

Justice is an essential value because it affects liberty, individual freedom and equality. All are essential in personal, social, or political contexts and necessary for the concept of goodness to exist and prevail.

Basically, there are three kinds of freedom. One is a natural freedom people possess as human beings in relationship with others. Being free to determine what one is going to do is a form of liberty. Another form of liberty is internal freedom: to be free from conflict within oneself and to become who one wants to be. In some cases, people must free themselves from others' expectations and needs in order to pursue their own dreams and passions. Dependence on others is not freedom or liberty. Eventually everybody has to face life alone in their solitude and inner self.

Society has faced coercion, where people are limited through physical or psychological force to meet the needs or demands of others. Autocratic governments and relationships can restrict people from meeting their potential and life's path. Their freedom is inhibited, and hope diminishes. Being independent, but also part of a whole, and finding one's path must endure if creativity and ideas are to survive.

Beauty concerns aesthetic sensibilities. Art and nature are generally the province of beauty, although mathematicians and scientists see the beauty of equations and theorems. Beauty exists in truth.

In many cases, beauty is considered subjective and reveals itself in experiences and art. Music, paintings, sculptures, relationships, and other phenomena provide metaphysical experiences that can touch the spirit and soul. Emotion and feeling come alive during aesthetic experiences, as they also do for scientists, philosophers, and naturalists.

Goodness concerns both truth and justice because they involve the "right course of action." Goodness involves the quality of relationships between people—that is, our "neighborly morality" and then ethical treatment of others.

Howard Gardner asserted, "I've come to see 'the good' as a property of our relations with other human beings—individuals whom we know well and also those who are unfamiliar; groups, both close and remote; and, less directly though equally importantly, individuals with whom we have relations as a result of our work or our membership in a profession. . . . I speak of good persons, good citizens, and good workers."[15]

In many respects, goodness has to do with the golden rule—"Do unto others . . . "—which concerns the common humanity between and among all human beings. The penchant to hyphenate people into distinct groups works against viewing each other as part of all humanity, deserving of respect and honor. As citizens, common humanity is served through the Bill of Rights and the judicial system and rule of law.

As a result, living ethically and pursuing truth, justice, liberty, equality, and goodness are essential. A well-educated individual will be ready for an undisclosed future and the changes it brings to society, individuals, and the economy.

Ethics and values are more important than ever with the rise of technology and its possible impact on democracy and human rights. One can be technologically proficient in an autocratic, immoral, and rigidified society. Free speech and social relationships are affected by technology and other changes. Life is more than science, technology, engineering, and mathematics. While they are important, the issues of truth, beauty, justice, liberty, and equality require more from individuals and society.

Philosophy and the humanities offer content but also avenues to higher thinking. Critical, complex, and skeptical thinking raise questions that are essential for individuals as well as society as a whole. Artists and poets are as important as scientists and mathematicians in providing a life of goodness, curiosity, creativity, and morality. Raising the human spirit is more important to "being" than simply "doing" in life.

Big Questions

The big questions in life
Come wrapped in simple covers,
Often unnoticed and invisible
Harking to the voices within us
That we have not heard or listened to
As we tread through the tangible world.
Like a time-release capsule, those queries
Fill our veins slowly, almost unnoticeably,
With the bittersweet nectar of change, flowing
Unperceptively until through spontaneous combustion
They melt our masks and betray our childlike honesty that
Hid in the mind's inner forest, tied in the velvet chains of
The expectations and compliance imposed by others.
Breaking those soft chains is a silent act
Taking place in the placid ponds
Of mind and soul that erupts
Tidal waves, coloring the world in
New and unexpected hues of passion.
That passion changes the eyes of others
Who now see you, unblurred by
Those things that give happiness or pain,
Lifting the veil of approval that divides
And makes us mirrors of each other.

WHAT TO REMEMBER

- Conflict exists between doing and being. Being involves staying in the present, accepting self and others for what they are and not for what they do. Acceptance, compassion, inclusion, and care are "being" values.
- Conformism works against finding a sense of self and identity.

- "Presence" combines sensing (seeing future possibilities) and presence (being in the present moment).
- Presencing involves focusing on what we want to bring into reality, suspending old habits of thought, and restricting the voice of judgment. Presencing helps new ideas and perspectives to come forth.
- Self-reflection doesn't come easy, but it is important to maintaining integrity and credibility. A major issue is understanding one's values, principles, and ethics.
- Ethics and virtue require individuals to look beyond self-interest and respect the dignity of others.
- Standing on principle is living up to values and commitments, not going with the crowd and desiring ego-based recognition.
- Education is a search for truth internally and externally in the world and society.
- Finding a sense of self and calling nurtures creativity.

NOTES

1. Wilber, Ken, *Grace and Grit* (Boston: Shambhala Publications, 2000), 58.

2. Palmer, Parker, *Let Your Life Speak* (San Francisco: Jossey-Bass Publishers, 2000), 4–5.

3. Csikszentmihalyi, Mihaly, *The Evolving Self* (New York: Harper Perennial Publishers, 1993), 219.

4. Senge, Peter M., et al., *Presence: An Exploration of Profound Change in People, Organizations, and Society* (New York: Crown Publishing Group, 2005), 189, Kindle.

5. Senge et al., *Presence*, 230.

6. Scharmer, C. Otto, and Kaufer, Katrin, *Leading from the Emerging Future: From Ego-System to Eco-System Economies* (San Francisco: Berrett-Koehler Publishers, 2013), loc. 337–84, Kindle.

7. Singer, Irving, *Meaning in Life* (New York: Free Press, 1992), 43.

8. Hostetler, Karl, Macintyre Latta, Margaret A., and Sarroub, Loukia K., "Retrieving Meaning in Teacher Education: The Question of Being," Digital-Commons@University of Nebraska–Lincoln, May 14, 2007, http://digitalcommons.unl.edu/teachlearnfacpub/26.

9. Gomes, Peter J., *The Good Life: Truths That Last in Times of Need* (New York: HarperCollins, 2009), 39–40, Kindle.

10. Costa, John Dalia, *The Ethical Imperative* (Reading, MA: Perseus Books, 1988), 71.

11. Goens, George A., *It's Not My Fault: Victim Mentality and Becoming Response-able* (Lanham, MD: Rowman & Littlefield Publishers, 2017), 57, Kindle.

12. Adler, Mortimer, *How to Think about the Great Ideas: From the Great Books of Western Civilization* (Chicago: Open Court, 2000), 4, Kindle.

13. Adler, Mortimer, *Great Ideas* (New York: Macmillan, 1992), 868.

14. Adler, *How to Think about the Great Ideas*, 22.

15. Gardner, Howard, *Truth, Beauty, and Goodness Reframed: Educating for the Virtues in the Age of Truth in the Age of Truthiness and Twitter* (New York: Basic Books, 2011), 40, Kindle.

11

COURAGE, CREATIVITY, AND JOY

The most regretful people on earth are those who felt the call to creative work, who felt their own creative power restive and uprising, and gave to it neither power nor time.

—Mary Oliver

Success is not final, failure is not fatal: it is the courage to continue that counts.

—Winston Churchill

It takes courage to grow up and become who you really are.

—e. e. cummings

What propels a person to act in ways that others may think is dangerous either physically or to personal reputation? What is the motive? Why do some people step up front to take a position that will bring them controversy or spend time on projects or passions that seem to have no fiscal or prestige reward? Why sacrifice position, wealth, or well-being? It is all because of intangibles.

While life is filled with tangibles, in actuality, intangibles are what are critically important and what life is about. They are beyond the material realm and have no physical manifestation. Even in business, the intangibles of brand or reputation and customer satisfaction are keystones.

The human mind itself is an intangible. Intangible images, mental images stored in memory, deal with ideas, attitudes, perceptions, and imagination. Intangibles—integrity, fortitude, compassion, self-efficacy, and wisdom—are important in life. These build a foundation for relationships and garner respect and emotional connection. Creativity and courage, while mental and intangible, are revealed through actions. Joy and passion emanate from them as well as from events and activities.

However, not all intangibles are positive. Some are destructive and actually bury purpose and aspirations. They become visible in various ways. Resentment, for example, causes individuals to express themselves harshly. Bitterness toward others accompanies active- or passive-aggressive postures toward others.

Other negative emotions include jealousy, animosity, blaming, and anxiety. The lack of self-forgiveness or the forgiveness of others creates a burden, because these feelings cause people to sit on the shelf and not venture out to pursue opportunities and possibilities. Most negative emotions are "all about me," freezing people in their tracks and preventing them from being open to learn new things.

POSITIVE EMOTIONS

Positive emotions have a heartening impact on life's passion and meaning and help individuals face challenges in the future, while negative emotions curtail progress. According to George Vaillant, "I hold that we do not have to be taught positive emotions. Our brain is hardwired to generate them. Humanity's task is to pay attention to them, for they are the source of our spiritual being and the key to our cultural evolutionary progress."[1]

Parents and teachers certainly want children to develop positive attitudes. A major one is curiosity, which keeps individuals engaged throughout life, moving forward and opening new doors. Another is integrity, which creates trust and is extremely important in relationships.

Actions and words must be in harmony. Dreams don't become reality by a lightning strike from the clouds. Magic wands do not exist in life. A work ethic and fortitude are both essential for progress and success, along with a spirit of collaboration that is necessary to work with others. In a business study, critical factors for failure or success centered on an appropriate work culture fostering collaboration and commitment to common goals that are rooted in trustworthy leadership.

The key issue is trust, which is essential in fostering and sustaining loyal relationships. "Trust is a fragile, relational asset, formed by a combination of rational and affective or emotional elements."[2] Relationships rest on trust. They fail when it is lost and thrive when it is evident. Many so-called leaders are cognitively intelligent but cannot build trusting relationships based on respect and integrity. Egocentrism or fear gets in the way.

Finally, there are really no shortcuts. The virtue of patience is necessary. Most valuable things in life require patience—the time and effort necessary for creating a product or developing a long-term loving relationship. Children often wrongly think that great athletes or accomplishments are developed overnight.

Achievement takes effort and time; often the work and commitment that lead to achievement go unseen and unrecognized. What is not observed are the internal battles one has to confront in the presence of doubt or insecurity. Success and finding oneself involve work and dogged dedication—knowing one's passion, or calling, and pursuing it with patience and grit. Success emanates from passion and resolve in all facets of life. It buffers failure and fuels the energy to continue and pursue purpose.

Passion concerns love and the conscious feelings of respect, appreciation, acceptance, sympathy, empathy, compassion, tenderness, and gratitude.[3] Vaillant affirms that love is not simply about words; it is about being able to accept and take love in, but it also is about the need to be able to give love back.

Compassion is closely linked to love. While love is based on attachment, compassion revolves around empathy, which is the ability to "resonate with another's pain, but to do something about it."[4] It is also a facet of forgiveness, which requires releasing negative judgments and feelings toward another.

A future wants to unfold, and clinging to a past with resentments and hurt impedes it from emerging. Only when past resentments or hurts are released can joy then be found in pursuing life in terms of the interests and talents that connect individuals to themselves, to others, and to their mission.

Passion and commitment nurture courage. Courage, creativity, and joy seem to be discrete concepts, but in reality, they are connected and there is an ebb and flow between them.

Anyone confronting uncertainty in life requires decisions about what actions, if any, are necessary to address it, in addition to exploring the possibility of new perspectives or approaches. Creativity may be required rather than simply following a set or established pattern. Success in highly difficult times is an intense emotional and joyful experience. Addressing issues in accord with values and principles brings a sense of joy at achieving goals and overcoming obstacles and limitations.

Joy emanates from acting courageously and creatively to maintain or generate a meaningful course or outcome. Uncertainties can be hedgerows to finding success and understanding and the ability to live one's life. Living with integrity to one's values and standards reinforces a sense of self and meaning.

Overcoming fear and anxiety requires courage. Fear emanates from not living or measuring up to the standards of society or profession or the expectations of others. The fear of loss, illness, or death also concerns people. Fear produces the anxiety of doubt, guilt, and failure, and anxiety is the fear of the unknown and doubt about the future. Heading into the unknown is not easy.

Fear also emanates from a sense of helplessness, which "is the enemy of happiness."[5] An important aspect of happiness is having a sense of control. Many children and adults have a fear of helplessness and do not feel free to shift their decisions and change their behavior. Not sensing such freedom blocks their decisions and pursuit of happiness.

Individuals cannot hide from these feelings. They must address them and confront their self-doubts and fear of failure. Wallowing in self-pity is self-destructive. All people contend with some turmoil in their lives—it is inevitable—but letting it cement one in place only fosters greater anxiety.

In addition, letting go of old baggage and perspectives is necessary. The past is gone, and the future begins now. Moving in a new or courageous direction involves risk. Things that are not essential must be released, and barriers to moving forward must be removed. To do so, minds must open and see what is emerging more clearly. "Letting go and surrendering can be thought of as two sides of the same coin. Letting go concerns the opening process, the removal of barriers and junk in one's way, and surrendering is moving into the resulting open-ing."[6]

Everyone has attachments: the need for approval and competence or the need to maintain strict independence from others. These two at-tachments can cause individuals to resist trying something new. The need for approval causes people to "play it safe" and protect their own self-image. Attachments, as the word implies, are important in decision-making and can keep individuals in place or spur activity in new direc-tions, depending on the nature of the attachment.

COURAGE

Courage, of course, is necessary. In complex situations, information may not be accessible. There are unknowns and uncertainties. As Don-ald Rumsfeld, former secretary of Defense infamously stated, "Reports that say that something hasn't happened are always interesting to me, because as we know, there are known knowns; there are things we know we know. We also know there are known unknowns; that is to say we know there are some things we do not know."[7] Events and circum-stances can be disorienting, and often people feel they are on new or unfamiliar ground. Addressing complex and confusing times takes forti-tude and resolve.

Psychologist Rollo May had this to say about courage:

> Courage is the capacity to meet the anxiety which arises as one achieves freedom. . . . The hallmark of courage in our age of confor-mity is the capacity to stand on one's own convictions—not obsti-nately or defiantly (these are expressions of defensiveness not cou-rage) nor as a gesture of retaliation, but simply because these are what one believes. It is as though one were saying through one's actions, "This is myself, my being." Courage is the affirmative choice, not a choice because "I can do no other"; for if one can do no other, what courage is involved?[8]

Every life has moments, some large and others seemingly small, that call for action to preserve a sense of self—who one is as an individual human being. When they arise, the significance of the issue can be felt in the chest as well as the mind. Breathing changes and the intensity of feeling increases as values and principles collide with the conditions and circumstances of life.

Whyte examined the concept of courage. He wrote, "The word courage arises from the old French cuer, meaning heart. Courageousness means at bottom to be heartfelt. To begin with we take only those steps which we can do in a heartfelt fashion and then slowly increase our stride as we become familiar with the direct connection between our passion and our courage."[9]

Society has a distorted view of heroism. People always think it is an act of daring in the face of physical conflict or difficulty. Certainly heroes may help people to safety in times of tragedy. There are many examples: when soldiers save a buddy from death in combat, when people jump into a torrential river to save someone from drowning, or when police or firefighters save individuals in times of extreme crisis.

While there is physical courage, there is also moral courage based on principles. Following a road less traveled and sometimes going against the grain on beliefs or positive values and ethics constitute living a life of heroism. Being courageous is generally perceived as bravery in the face of potential pain or physical threat. But courage also relates to acting with honor and moral fortitude and goodness in matters of the heart and soul. Behaving in a heartfelt manner to do what is right—sincerely, earnestly, and with passion—takes courage. Courage in this sense does not often garner the limelight. Sometimes it is done in silent solitude.

Looking inside and learning about self fashion individuals' reactions and mindsets. Internal perceptions and what and how people feel affect attitudes, actions, and, importantly, how circumstances are perceived and assessed.

Senator John McCain indicated that courage is not always comprehensible. There is an emotional aspect of life that sets the foundation for courage to emerge. He stated, "It's love, then, that makes courage necessary. And it's love that makes courage possible for all of us to possess."[10] Love of country, family, friends, and values stir the motivation to act, to stand up and protect them.

Courage is acting on behalf of what is noble. In this regard, individuals sacrifice pleasure, happiness, and their present existence for what is good and noble.

Tillich stated, "Man is what he makes of himself. And the courage to be oneself is the courage to make of himself what one wants to be."[11] That implies that to be courageous, one must know oneself, one's principles, values, standards, and calling. Individuals must have the courage "to be"—to affirm their true selves, who they are, and what they stand for. Courage is required because there are others who want them to be different—to fit into the mold that others think is right for them.

Moral courage is based on moral principles and includes the risk of unpopularity, position, and status. Perseverance and honesty are requisite: speaking one's truth, taking responsibility, and enduring criticism. Acting with integrity to values and ethics takes resolve and bravery.

Courage is also evident over time in relationships that demand increasing commitment and openness. Investing in connections with others and balancing independence requires sacrifice. Putting oneself on record clearly allows others to know what values are at the essence of personal decisions. The fear of losing autonomy and independence requires courageous decisions. Individuals must confront their fear of abandonment and the need for dependence on others.

Creativity and love free the soul. Connections with others in love and friendship help individuals to see themselves more clearly and provide a needed sense of acceptance by others. Loneliness can be debilitating at all ages. People must live with themselves and with others. Finding oneself may become apparent through relationships with other people as well as through the internal passions that cry for expression through and within each individual.

Living a heroic life requires doing what is right even if it means personal sacrifice and speaking boldly on principle for those who have no voice. Being the voice in the wilderness calling out for justice and fairness when others stand silent is a heroic act.

Vaclav Havel indicated, "We are still incapable of understanding that the only genuine core of all our actions—if they are to be moral—is responsibility. Responsibility to something higher than my family, my country, my firm, my success. Responsibility to the order of Being, where all our actions are indelibly recorded and where, and only where, they will be properly judged."[12]

CREATIVITY AND COURAGE

Another form of courageous decision-making involves creativity, which involves taking the lead and engaging in new and different paths. Leaders with a new vision are courageous because they break the mold of a perceived fixed future. They address future threats and anticipate and recognize the issues and implications before they are universally recognized. Every profession requires some creative courage to promote new ideas, direction, and vision.

"Creative courage" is different from moral courage. Moral courage concerns established principle and doing the right thing, while creative courage, in contrast, involves pursuing new forms, new symbols, or new patterns to address current or future issues. Individuals who have creative courage see shifts in the landscape and identify patterns and dynamics that are going to affect the organization and people within it. They synthesize ideas and elements from other professions and apply them to their work to meet impending challenges.

Confidence is required to break new ground, but it should not be confused with rashness. Charging ahead with bluster and ego can lead to disaster. Courageous people have conviction but also the fortitude to recognize their doubts and still move forward and grow. Being ahead of one's time produces criticism: people may not understand what is emerging, and one's decisions can be perceived as implausible or "out of touch" with reality.

Imagination sets people apart from other creatures and living things. Imagination "is the power to bring to mind things that are not present to our senses."[13] Through imagination, children and others release their minds from the present and spring into the past to revisit times of yore, or they examine the present and its curiosities and issues, or they look to the future and contemplate life and the universe.

Imagination is the foundation for creativity and ingenious and inspired thinking. Originality springs from imagination: seeing things with new eyes, speculating, and hypothesizing all bring forth different perspectives and options. Making new or diverse connections spurs different approaches to breaking out of the mold or regimen.

Divergent, out-of-the-box ideas break the strict regimen of moving through a set of prescribed rules or regulations. Intuition is at work, as are feelings and emotions. Poets, artists, and others must master their craft, but emotions and dedication push them to create in new and different ways. New perspectives lead to creative ventures. "Creative work also reaches deep into our intuitive and unconscious minds and into our hearts and feelings."[14]

Too often, people think that creativity is only the domain of special people or geniuses and that it only resonates in certain fields such as the fine arts or design. But in reality, it is necessary in all facets of life: business, science, education, and relationships.

Creativity is not a have-or-have-not proposition: it is false to assume that individuals either have it or they don't. Creativity does not occur at a fixed rate. Intelligence and knowing things are connected to creativity, and having deep background information and knowledge can spur examining issues from different perspectives.

Creativity is indifferent to time. It evolves at different rates, from slow evolution to sudden "aha" moments of quick insight or realization. Creativity involves peaks and valleys and is not simply a smooth, linear process. Sometimes things move incrementally but very slowly. That process provides intuitive insights as well as epiphanies when things that seem fractured coalesce together.

However, creativity can be stifled. Simply focusing on recall, binary thinking, and a closed mindset will stymie the creativity within children as well as adults. The voice of judgment also suppresses creativity. To some degree, everyone is creative, but the conformist pressures of society and peer groups can restrict creativity. Groupthink and censoring ideas and approaches are detrimental to originality.

At work, people can be limited in finding new ways in different approaches if the corporate or business culture is closed. Open-mindedness and critical thinking can keep a business relationship productive and fulfilling. Individuals find meaning in organizations in which they can contribute for the sake of a serious purpose or cause.

Julia Cameron indicated that creativity exists within an aura of safety, optimism, and hope. She asserted that creativity, at heart, is about play, because imagination needs to be free to play with ideas and perspectives.

As in every aspect of life, there are times of high passion, and times of cold indifference. Creativity requires humility to continue, begin again, start anew. In doing so, "the process of identifying a self inevitably involves loss as well as gain. We discover our boundaries, and those boundaries by definition separate us from our fellows. As we clarify our perceptions, we lose our misconceptions. As we eliminate ambiguity, we lose illusion as well. We arrive at clarity, and clarity creates change."[15]

A critical issue is self-acceptance. Without it, creativity lies dormant. "Self-care is the oxygen of creativity. Self-love is a healing rain and nurturing sun. Self-care and self-love begin with self-acceptance that is grounded in self-knowledge."[16]

That all individuals are unique actually emanates from them in their perspectives, ideas, and approaches to life. All people have a small voice of creativity that moves them in finding and pursuing aspirations. That is why children should listen to what calls them and not always pay attention to the chatter of society and peer groups or the expectations of others.

All individuals have something to live for; purpose provides meaning, and meaning provides the satisfaction and energy to contribute to something greater than themselves. What they live for defines the relevance of their lives far more than simply acquiring sustenance and material goods. Actually, it is the opportunity to learn, grow, and contribute to others that provides meaning and happiness.

JOY

Joy is related to creativity and curiosity. Children see the joy in birds nesting, the work of a bee on a summer flower, and the appearance of their mother or father after a business trip out of town. Joy involves the element of surprise and curiosity. Life presents mysteries and surprises, and having them revealed is a joyful experience.

Joy is a spiritual experience that involves a connection to others as well as a connection to the universe. A reunion with a loved one is joyous. Seeing nature at work in the various seasons brings joy. Listening to music brings emotion and joy. Joy is also watching children play and act and certainly comes from being there when children take their first step or say their first word.

Joy also exists in the emotional expression of saying yes to one's true identity. Knowing and understanding "Who am I?" is a joyful experience and an expression of a unique and fulfilling life.

The Soul

The soul stands alone
Separate from the gray
Light of thought.
Blanching against reason
It echoes the past,
The time before we arrived
In our bundled blankets.
The soul is the heart's
Reflection,
The synchronous partner,
The soft receptacle
of intuition and wisdom.

WHAT TO REMEMBER

- Intangibles are powerful in relationships and life. They build a foundation for relationships, motivation, and courage.
- Confronting uncertainty requires creativity and courage to overcome fear and anxiety and let go of attachments.
- Creativity involves an active curiosity to explore and engage with new and different paths and approaches. Confidence is necessary to understand shifts and patterns and dynamics in order to break new ground.
- Imagination sets people apart from other creatures and is the foundation for creativity. Creativity requires humility to try to begin again. In everyone, there is a voice of creativity that can move them.
- Joy is a spiritual experience and is related to creativity, curiosity, and self.

NOTES

1. Vaillant, George E., *Spiritual Evolution* (New York: Broadway Books, 2008), 17.

2. Savolainen, T., and P. Lopez-Fresno, "Trust as Intangible Asset: Enabling Intellectual Capital Development by Leadership for Vitality and Innova-

tiveness," *Electronic Journal of Knowledge Management* 11, no. 3, 244–55, http://www.ejkm.com/issue/download.html?idArticle=407.

3. Vaillant, *Spiritual Evolution*, 16.

4. Vaillant, *Spiritual Evolution*, 155.

5. Dozier, Rush, Jr., *Fear Itself* (New York: Thomas Dunne Books, 1998), 223.

6. Scharmer, C. Otto, *Theory U.* (Cambridge, MA: Society for Organizational Learning, 2007), 185.

7. Rumsfeld, Donald, "DoD News Briefing," February 12, 2002, http://archive.defense.gov/Transcripts/Transcript.aspx?TranscriptID=2636.

8. May, Rollo, *Man's Search for Himself* (New York: W. W. Norton & Company, 2009), 169–78.

9. Whyte, David, *Crossing the Unknown Sea* (New York: Riverhead Books, 2001), 14.

10. McCain, John, *Why Courage Matters* (New York: Random House, 2004), 203.

11. Tillich, Paul, *The Courage to Be* (New Haven, CT: Yale University Press, 1952), 150.

12. Havel, Vaclav, *The Art of the Impossible* (New York: Knopf Publishers, 1991), 19.

13. Robinson, Ken, *The Element* (New York: Viking Publishers, 2009), 58.

14. Robinson, *Element*, 79.

15. Cameron, Julia, and Mark Bryan, *The Artists Way* (New York: G. P. Putnam's Sons), 81.

16. Cameron and Bryan, *Artists Way*, 238.

12

HEARTFELT WISDOM

To know thyself is the beginning of wisdom.

—Socrates

Without freedom of thought, there can be no such thing as wisdom—and no such thing as public liberty without freedom of speech.

—Benjamin Franklin

An ignorant man is always able to say yes or no immediately to any proposition. To a wise man, comparatively few things can be propounded which do not require a response with qualifications, with discriminations, with proportion.

—Horace Mann

The decisions people make shape their lives. Choices are not always easy, because decision points unfold over time from childhood through old age. Judgments, both subtle and large, create the platform for potential destinies to unfold. What decisions to make and how and why to make them are all-important.

All people face similar challenges, but each is framed with individual distinctiveness emotionally, intellectually, and philosophically. Similar circumstances viewed from individual perspectives result in diverse approaches, decisions, and outcomes. Despite experiencing the same times and collective events, interpretations and desires create totally different lives. Fate, serendipity, relationships, as well as the choices of others, also define one's life. No one has complete or total control of life and destiny.

One certain thing waits for everyone: death. The road between birth and death is uncertain and varies; the path is not the same for everyone except that it ends. With this reality, the essence and experience of life must be savored and maximized for each person's distinctive pathway.

Everyone dies—but does everyone live? Fred Kofman indicated that death is a teacher and that people should confront their mortality in order to live fully. He wrote, "Dying before you die is the hardest and most important work that you can do if you want to truly live and truly lead. It does not require that you face death in a literal sense, but it does mean that you have to look deeply at your own life and its inevitable end and realize that everyone around you is on the same lifeboat."[1]

People like to think about beginnings, not endings. Some find it morbid. While the end cannot be planned, life itself plays out by decisions and reacting to situations and opportunities. As mentioned earlier, Viktor Frankl stated that people are free under any and all circumstances to decide how they react mentally and spiritually to conditions. Living is engaging with situations—it is not stagnant or a prewritten play.

Kofman also stated that because people are mortal, they should focus "on what truly matters: truth, happiness, meaning, love, friendship, gratitude, awe, compassion, peace, fullness, and freedom."[2] There is little time, and living enthusiastically and facing life's trials and tribulations is the pathway to those matters.

Sleepwalking through life and adopting a victim mentality in response to difficult conditions or the actions of others is a dead end. Others distract themselves and focus on trivial matters and pursuits devoid of substance and meaning. The ego dominates, and people lose track of their true selves in the forest of narcissism.

LIVING LIFE

Individuals only have one life to live. Not engaging consciously in the world with its risks and opportunities is not a benign judgment. In retirement years some individuals despair that their lives might have been richer indicating, "I could have" or "If I would have." Retrospect sometimes presents a clearer picture of decisions than did the actual time in which they were made, but time does not wait, life happens today, and each person is in charge of his or her own potential and outcomes.

Comfort sometimes limits opportunity. As noted earlier, apprehension is an issue. Some are concerned with what they can lose, not with what they can gain. The security of the known, even if it is uncomfortable, usurps the appeal of adventure. Not deciding is a decision, too, and circumvents any potential or new opportunities. In the aftermath and as time passes, those individuals reflect on their decision not to decide; then "What if?" questions are raised with no real answers.

The richness of life is found in finding meaning and love through compassion, following one's mission, and appreciating the beauty of the natural order. Each person has an inner voice—a soul—that speaks and raises issues affecting his or her destiny and potential. While complexity and complications can blur perspective, the heart and intuitive values and principles provide insight and direction.

A good life based on principle and values is more directly related to finding meaning than one focused solely on financial security or recognition. Too often, people fall for the manipulation of consumerism and material goods and external intangibles rather than emphasizing the richness of creativity, nature, and pursuing a desired destiny.

Meaning includes making sense of life (cognition) and having a sense of purpose (motivation), which are achieved through helping others and contributing to community and society.[3] Self-absorption is hollow and isolating and will not bring the satisfaction that individuals ultimately seek.

In the testimonials at ceremonies for those who died, the term "a good life" is frequently used. What does that mean? No life is stress-free or devoid of challenges and grief. Goodness has more to do with values than worldly assets.

Those living a good life have a sense of virtue and principle, with conscience directing them in the right and honorable direction. They are good neighbors who are helpful, considerate, and respectful. Honesty, trustworthiness, and civility are at the core of their character. A good person can be relied upon to show up when the need arises, to apply reason and logic to situations, and to help others find answers. They also realize matters of the heart and demonstrate love and compassion to others as human beings deserving of respect and understanding.

Fulfilling obligations to others is important. Goodwill flows to others and is part of the moral imperative in life. Thomas Sergiovanni, in the book *Moral Leadership,* stated, "Certain ideals enhance human life and assist people in fulfilling their obligations to one another. These should be served whenever possible. Among the most important ideals are . . . tolerance, compassion, loyalty, forgiveness, peace, brotherhood, justice (giving people their due), and fairness (being impartial, as opposed to favoring selected people)."[4]

Society today can be devoid of these ideals. Civility gets lost in instant social media messages. Individuals live in technological and philosophical silos. Logic, understanding, and compassion are suppressed by anger and arrogance. Temperance disappears, and prudence and self-control are erased from media that are focused on ego and swagger. Good manners, tolerance, and personal responsibility get lost. Society becomes harsher and divisive. Bitterness and thoughtlessness are evident in politics and social media and, unfortunately, in everyday life. Disrespectful actions are displayed in all contexts, including the media, the halls of Congress, and the executive branch of government in both harsh and subtle ways.

Thomas Merton advised, "To allow oneself to be carried away by a multitude of conflicting concerns, to surrender to too many demands, to commit oneself to too many projects, to want to help everyone in everything, is to succumb to violence. The frenzy of our activism neutralizes our work for peace. It destroys our own inner capacity for peace. It destroys the fruitfulness of our own work, because it kills the root of inner wisdom which makes work fruitful."[5] Being distracted by harried social disruptions can be immobilizing. Finding direction and passion provides solid ground for addressing issues.

A civil society demands more from individuals in their actions and reactions to others. The character traits of courage, humanity, temperance, justice, and transcendence must be developed and modeled. Society and family require them if people are to live respectfully and wisely and nurture the values of respect and compassion. Character, however, begins with each individual.

Going inside oneself is necessary at times. Constant external noise and continuous blasts of information and opinion create cacophony and pressure. Finding peace is not easy. Living constantly in the swell of ego and social and professional expectations can frustrate and deaden feelings and insight. Individuals lose sight of themselves while looking down the external road of expectations and demands. The "doings" of life overcome the "beings" of life—and individuals lose focus about who they are and who they desire to be.

Finding a sense of being requires silence from the external dissonance of others' expectations and the internal clatter of uncertainties and insecurities. Taking time to silently reflect and clarify feelings and emotions opens the mind to awareness of one's needs and satisfaction.

Intuitiveness and imagination can be mobilized. There are times when both want to arise, but the demands of daily life get in the way and muffle or suppress those thoughts from coming forward. One's internal voice needs to be heard. Self-doubt amid the chaos of life can cast a debilitating shadow, but it can encourage self-reflection and determine what is authentic and what is contrived.

Being genuine is not easy among the pressures of work, family, and social networks. Keeping the "real self" visible requires resolve—coming to an understanding that self-awareness is more than one's outer image, titles, and roles—and each individual must be true to the real self, not to a manufactured or counterfeit one. Taking time for the things that bring joy and love nourishes the soul. Replenishing internal energy comes from creating a sense of wholeness inside and outside.

In all of this, people must live with integrity to who they are and to the principles on which they stand. After all, the self is constructed on a foundation of beliefs and principles. Honoring them leads to self-acceptance. Knowing one's weaknesses and strengths results in living with character, authenticity, and increased strength. Character and self-awareness go hand in hand.

Living honestly and with loyalty and wisdom leads to a sense of well-being. People can endure and thrive if they do the right things and live with integrity and responsibility to principles. Being true to oneself results in acceptance and peace.

Loyalty is one character quality that is often neglected, but it may actually provide guidance on life's path and direction. Loyalty to a cause or mission may be the answer to fulfillment because inside each individual are causes—in the realms of education, art, politics, equality, or religion—that inspire and direct one's life.

Loyalty can be toward a lifelong interest in a cause or ideal that requires consistent concern and action. However, there are good and bad causes: some develop around noble ideas, respect, and understanding and create a sense of community. Others push divisiveness and separation. Loyalty to positive values builds relationships with others to enhance the common good, in which a sense of unity and meaning develops. Predatory loyalty stifles the greater story to be told and fulfilled by the community and individuals.

All of this requires making the most of the time people have and meeting their sense of possibility. Meaning, purpose, and noble ventures move beyond a life of self-interest to one of satisfaction and community. Contributions to something larger than oneself is fulfilling and important.

Principles are like duties or rules that serve as guiding standards for a good life.[6] They are basic truths or assumptions that apply to personal, social, and professional situations. Principles contribute to the welfare of the individuals holding them, as well as to others and society in general.

Virtues are similar to character traits. A person of virtue does the right thing under all circumstances. In life, situations arise that are complicated or unclear but require a decision. At times, what is right is not always clearly evident; sometimes there are two propositions, both of which have virtue. Those who act on them may alienate others and create conflict over what is "right." Standing still without acting on questions of character or rightness is still an action, and it affects people internally and externally: they lose integrity with others and they create a sense of failure within themselves.

HEARTS

Each person's heart floats above time, immune to seconds, minutes, and hours. Calendars and clocks cannot affect hearts—they are timeless. They are not mechanical parts or technical instruments, and their depth cannot be measured by tests or gizmos but only by life's actions. They are the soul's beacons.

People say, for example, "She [or he] has a big heart." That's true for most people, even if their hearts have been broken a few times. Hearts hold love, memories, and dreams. They are receptacles of loving memories, holding the people loved—past and present—in clear focus even when they are not present.

The heart crosses the boundaries of time and binds people together across generations and even centuries. The passion of great artists from a hundred years ago can be experienced. A sense of the emotions people felt decades ago under a given circumstance can be felt as if the event happened today. Hearts are tuned to fields of energy and feeling that exist in each individual today and everyone who came before.

A heartfelt connection cannot be broken. The time people have together lives forever in each of their souls. The force of nature cannot alter or change that, and no act of humankind can erase the feelings and memories created with others. When people have loving relationships, hearts beat as one and time becomes meaningless.

Some of the lessons of the heart are these:

- Be young at heart. Never lose childlike enthusiasm; be curious and have fun.
- Give heartfelt thanks. Always thank people for what they do, and do good things for others even if there are no thanks in return.
- Always have heart. Life is more than skills and knowledge. Great accomplishments come from people with "heart" who never gave up, never got discouraged, and always believed. Persevere!
- Remember your heart and soul. Express love to those around you. Love is infinite; it is the one thing that is unlimited and grows when you give it away.

Heartfelt connections reach beyond time and help individuals remember the past and create the future.

WISDOM

The word *wisdom* conjures up images of ancient times past. *Wisdom* seems like an impractical, very abstract, and philosophical word, one not related directly to work or life. It is something people discuss after a person's death or only in retrospect, of events and decisions many years back. The message seems to be that some people have it and others do not or ever will.

Wisdom, however, incorporates deep intelligence, knowledge, moral rectitude, heart, and soul. It is much more than rote intelligence and the regurgitation of facts, data, or theories. Simple recall or comprehension is not nearly sufficient. If it were, technology and machines would be wise.

Wisdom concerns what really matters and what is worthwhile. It has a direct link to judgment, perspective, and decisions. Principles, values, and ethics offer guiding lights and understanding. When looking at circumstances, wise people assess and judge and define and interpret appropriate information. They comb through statements, opinions, and data and determine what is truthful and consequential and significant based on moral integrity and imperatives. They can see subtle nuances that can be of great consequence.

Wise individuals see the heart of important issues, have insight into motives and behavior, and behave in a straightforward, compassionate manner. Their attitude is consistent with standards and ethical conduct.

Wise leaders' behavior is congruent with their knowledge and principles; they must live up to them or they lose their trustworthiness and honor. They have the capacity to listen and hear as well as see, examine, and remember.

According to Mihaly Csikszentmihalyi, wisdom has three different aspects. "In the first place, it is a way of knowing, or *cognitive skill.* Second, it is a special way of acting that is socially desirable, or a *virtue.* And finally it is a *personal good*, because the practice of wisdom leads to inner serenity and enjoyment. . . . These characteristics distinguish wisdom from other cognitive processes we may call '*intelligence*,' '*scientific knowledge*,' or '*genius*.'"[7]

In the realm of technology, there is artificial intelligence, but technology cannot provide "artificial wisdom"—hearts and minds are not programmable. Matters of ethics and values can be defined, but it takes a conscience and heart to apply them in complex human circumstances. Human wisdom, not algorithms, is required.

Wise individuals do not determine a course of action simply on the basis of what is the easiest or quickest option. They look to the future and maximize the well-being of themselves and others. Wisdom involves understanding that life involves more than what is always obvious and, at times, exceptions must be made to do what is right. At times, it requires courage and civic responsibility above comfort and ease.

The subject of wisdom was addressed by the philosophers of ancient Greece. *Philosophy*, in fact, is a combination of *philo* ("love") and *sophia* ("wisdom") that means "the love of wisdom."

Plato described three types of wisdom.[8] The first is *sophia*, having to do with contemplation and seeking life's truths. The second is *phronesis*, which concerns the experienced and practical wisdom of lawyers, judges, and government leaders. The third is *episteme*, the quality of seeking to understand the world through the lens of science.

All of these definitions imply that knowledge leads to a good life. It is not dependent upon obtaining a college degree. Obviously, thinking and reasoning are necessary, as is coming to terms with conditions and circumstances. Complacency is not a facet of wisdom; it impedes individuals from contemplative action, even in the face of others' demands and expectations.

Wisdom has its perils and demands. Individuals who stand up to be counted on philosophical grounds may pay the price of ridicule, loss of relationships, castigation, and even legal action. Courage is necessary to living with wisdom, which can involve seeing and challenging what others distort, ignore, or misunderstand.

Sometimes individuals in difficult and traumatic health or other circumstances find a greater understanding of life and a sense of wisdom. Many individuals, after moving through the travails of a health problem, indicate that they have greater compassion for others, increased capacity for forgiveness and humility, and a deeper understanding of the ambiguous nature of things. In other words, they acquire deeper insight and wisdom into the human condition and what makes for a good life. Trivialities and escapism fade.

Education has always been the vehicle to wisdom. It requires a foundation in knowledge and complex thinking. Unfortunately, today, many schools do not speak of wisdom, as they are consumed by technology and career education. While there is a question as to whether wisdom can be taught, knowledge and thinking are starting points, along with an understanding of values and principles and the intangibles of heart and soul. Philosophy does matter, because it concerns ideas, beliefs, ethics, and ideological viewpoints.

One facet of education should be reading philosophy and classical literature. They can provide the basis for discussion concerning points of view and perspectives. In addition, students must decipher truth from opinion or false perspectives. Skeptical stances can create discussion and thought. Understanding different philosophical dispositions can result in comprehending others' points of view and arguments. Philosophy offers a window into how others think and perceive life at its unfolding.

Robert Steinberg identified principles for teaching to help children develop wisdom.[9] Wisdom includes a balance. Certainly, knowing what one knows and does not know is essential. Many people do not realize that the unknown can have an essential, possibly devastating, impact on their choices and decisions. Wise individuals are adaptable and able to maintain balance in their actions in different environments and circumstances. They are mindful and considerate.

Wise people are not fearful of changing their minds as knowledge, experience, and circumstances dictate. They make judgments that are clear and sensible and keep in mind the short- and long-term consequences of them. Wise people learn from their mistakes, as well as from those of others. Ego does not get in the way of judgment.

Analytical thinking skills can be taught in a variety of content areas. Evaluating information and forming judgments are important, but so is dialogical thinking—seeing problems from a variety of perspectives, not just one. Too often, only one perspective is presented, and understanding alternative perspectives is lost. At times, those with minority standpoints may demonstrate wisdom and virtue that provide answers when answers are needed.

Comprehending how others see a problem from a different viewpoint than one's own is necessary in a society that engages in free speech and collaborative decision-making. The paradigms for thinking are not static and may change with time. Students should have to make the case for positions that are philosophically different from their own in order to truly understand their own point of view.

Wisdom requires developing a set of values to think critically, creatively, and rationally, all of which are necessary to achieve "good" ends. Wise individuals comprehend how positive ideas can produce negative ends. For example, to limit social conflict and abrasive language, people will suggest that some forms of speech be limited. Expression of ideas is repressed. In such cases, harsh expression may be curtailed, but freedom of speech is limited, which can lead to greater oppression.

Wise people apply knowledge to create a better world, not one that violates individual freedom and speech in order to meet the will of the majority. Sometimes what the majority favors can lead to its own demise. Responding to brutish taunts with the restriction of the rights of others destroys the very freedom individuals need to curtail uncivil or unwise behavior.

In addition, defining the different perspectives of the common good and the basis for their interpretation are important. Various perspectives exist for the common good. Finding options for actions and values—good and bad—and their reasons and circumstances highlight potential abuses and opportunities. Action should be based on knowledge, experience, and understanding, which require ethical, academic, and moral judgment.

> We don't receive wisdom; we must discover it for ourselves after a
> journey that no one can take for us or spare us.
>
> —Marcel Proust

Hearts

The dance of life moves
in the heartbeats that
pulse through the rivers
of our being.
Our hearts throb with stilted
rhythm when broken
by sorrow spilling from
the well of love.
The shroud of sorrow
leadens the heart's tempo,
slowing our motion so
we feel the eternal beauty of love's light.
Through that light
relationships become heart-felt,
filled with the passion and love
that heals and makes us whole.
Loving hearts calm life's storms
and gives us a glimpse of
heaven-sent grace that binds us

together beyond the illusion of time.

WHAT TO REMEMBER

- Everyone dies, but does everyone live? To truly live, individuals must focus on those things that matter in order to find meaning.
- A good life requires a sense of virtue applied through conscience and heartfelt understanding of others and principles.
- Finding a sense of self requires individuals to go inside of themselves away from social clatter, ego, and external expectations.
- Finding meaning requires loyalty, not only to others but also to principles and causes and positive values.
- Hearts are both tangible and intangible. The intangible heart holds love, memories, and dreams and binds people together in a sense of goodness. The tangible heart beats and keeps blood flowing through the body, but the intangible heart touches people's souls.
- Wisdom incorporates intelligence, knowledge, heart, moral rectitude, and soul in examining life's issues and complexities and reflects itself in decisions and behavior.

NOTES

1. Kofman, Fred, *The Meaning Revolution: The Power of Transcendent Leadership* (New York: Crown Publishing Group, 2018), 262, Kindle.

2. Kofman, *The Meaning Revolution*, 155.

3. Kofman, *The Meaning Revolution*, 21.

4. Sergiovanni, Thomas J., *Moral Leadership* (San Francisco: Jossey-Bass Publishers, 1992), 110.

5. Merton, Thomas, *Conjectures of a Guilty Bystander* (New York: Crown Publishing Group, 1966), 81.

6. Paterson, Sonja, et al., *Teaching Ethics: Care, Think and Choose: A Curriculum-Based Approach to Ethical Thinking* (Cheltenham, Victoria, Australia: Hawker Brownlow Education, 2011), loc. 151–207, Kindle.

7. Csikszentmihalyi, Mihaly, *The Evolving Self* (New York: Harper Perennial, 1993), 241–42.

8. Davis, Richard A., *The Intangibles of Leadership* (Hoboken, NJ: John Wiley and Sons, 2010) 4, Kindle.

9. Sternberg, Robert J., *Wisdom, Intelligence, and Creativity Synthesized* (Cambridge: Cambridge University Press, 2003), 160–66.

EPILOGUE

The value of life lies not in the length of days, but in the use we make of them. . . . Whether you find satisfaction in life depends not on your tale of years, but on your will.

—Michel de Montaigne

Autumn of Life

I sit in the late autumn of life
With the stirrings of spring singing in my soul, oblivious . . .
Oblivious to the weathered image in the morning mirror,
And to the dance of time and the reality of age.
There are days when I walk on colt's legs
Prancing on spirited limbs, filled
With the vibrant smells of life,
The bliss of emerging potential, and
The dreams of races to be won.
I feel caught,
Suspended in the illusion of time
Attached to the innocence of the past
Yet drawn to the rich pastures of cumulative years.
As youth pales
My shadow flows through browning pastures
Where grayed stallions with slowed gaits
Feed on the sweet and tart seeds of the past.
I live in the paradox of life.

Life unfolds continually across all stages, from childhood through old age. In a sense it's like a blank blackboard at birth waiting to be filled with the chalk of fate and each individual's choices.

The journey in life is to be experienced and celebrated. Live it! Don't just watch life go by—don't be a sluggish bystander. Participate! Carpe Diem! Seize the day! Become involved. Make a footprint in the sands of life and time!

Life is too precious to let it slip away watching others, seeking material comforts, searching for diversion, or trying to live your life to meet the expectations of others. Just as there are no duplicates, individuals should not let other people's expectations for them mold their own lives. Other people have their own life to live; they should not live other lives as well.

True bitterness comes from not making the effort to fulfill oneself. In that same vein, one must respect other people's lives, their journeys and their dreams. They must have the same liberty to follow their bliss as you do. Don't be controlling of others; each person has an individual mission in life.

When looking at life, there are three key principles to count on. First, cherish all life because it is a gift. Second, respect life because each person is as valuable as the next, and each sentient being is here for a reason. And, finally, protect life. Make wise decisions with regard to living things.

Life is to be cherished and not to be wasted or trivialized. Before committing life to ventures, make sure the decisions are wise—that there is a very compelling reason for acting on a new venture that honors life and protects it. Beware of those who use fear to convince others to engage in aggression and conflict.

In a nutshell, be a "steward of life," ensuring that people and the environment are in better shape because you were here.

- Wake-up! Don't sleepwalk through life. Stay awake and marvel at the wonder of the universe. Live each day as if it's your last, because some day it will be!
- Take a stand! There are great issues out there. Don't stand by and just observe. Be respectfully assertive. Question everything. Add to the debate. Some grave things happened in history because good people stood by, hoping someone else would act. Take a

stand and be known to the world. Be unique and authentic, not just an imitator or a lemming.

- Let go! Don't try to control everything; it's impossible anyway. Remember, don't do everything yourself and don't pull the sled on your own. Be kind to yourself. And remember, let other people contribute; everyone has talent and responsibilities and obligations.

- Live in the present! The past is gone. The future is not here. The only moment each person has is the one being lived now. The present moment is the only one guaranteed. Focus on it; be present in the present. Don't squander it! Fretting about the past is useless (and aggravating to others, and worrying about the future just produces anxiety). Living in the present also means recognizing every moment because each one is an invaluable opportunity.

- Find silence! Go sit under a tree! Observe the leaves, the sky, and the clouds. Enjoy the subtle sounds of the breeze. Listen to the life around you. Sit quietly. Feel the energy running through your body. Relax muscles, close eyes, and enjoy peace.

- Dream! Imagination is priceless and can provide you with great insight and joy. Peace in life is available if we recognize it. Silence is a spiritual gift to us all, allowing us to clear our minds and listen to our souls. Peace rests inside each of us, but we must take time to find it.

- Don't get caught up in worshiping technology as the cure for everything. Technology is simply a tool and comes with serious limitations and dysfunctions. The paradox is that while technology is to "connect" people digitally, it can isolate them socially and individually. The future is found in peaceful relationships and connections between people, not in flashy gizmos or technology.

- Technology doesn't provide happiness. People do. Technology will not help find the peace that awaits individuals in nature or in a moment of solitude. Virtual reality is not really reality, and peace cannot be found in computer chips or simulations.

- Listen! Stop talking! People talk too much and listen too little and get wrapped up with themselves. Listen to others. Really listen to the content and intent of what they are saying. Honor them by truly understanding what they have to say, their feelings, and the values and beliefs they hold.

- Listen to nature—the crickets, the bees, the grass blowing in the gentle wind, the call of birds, and the forlorn call of the coyotes at night. There's so much going on: listen and rejoice in it.
- Remember hearts and souls are sources of wisdom. Intuition—the whispering little voice—is saying something important. At times it's a warning and other times it's a call to freedom of choice and free will. Listen to intuition and respect it. But to use it, follow all of the earlier suggestions.
- Sometimes, do nothing! This is one of the hardest lessons to learn. Every now and then, people confuse motion with movement. It takes a wise person to know when to do nothing—to not meddle and just let things emerge. Every so often, when things are unclear and confusing, doing nothing is the right thing to do. Clarity comes with reflection and silence, and doing nothing is doing something, even if it rubs against our action-oriented society.
- Practice grace, not vanity! Ego is a big, big problem. Your ego can get you into a lot of trouble. People who have an inflated ego eventually explode and self-destruct. Grace, on the other hand, is a gift that respects others and yourself. Grace is the ability to handle situations with poise, dignity, and honor. It involves a deep sense of decency, kindness, mercy, and charity. Humility under the pressure of defeat or victory honors others and your own spirit.
- Forgive! This is life's hardest lesson. Learn to forgive people. People must also learn to forgive themselves.
- Always remember: common people achieve uncommon greatness. Only in America is there a "Fanfare for the Common Man." Aaron Copland wrote this wonderful music to recognize the spirit of the common person—listen to it. Underdogs can overcome all odds. The United States and the American Dream are built on this premise.

Finally, some simple words as reminders in facing life: Live! Feel! Learn! Love! Think! Give! Laugh! That last word is important: a good sense of humor, especially the ability to laugh at oneself, is a gift that can help people get through all kinds of situations gracefully.

BIBLIOGRAPHY

BOOKS

Adler, Mortimer. *Great Ideas*. New York: Macmillan Publishing, 1992.

Adler, Mortimer. *How to Think about the Great Ideas: From the Great Books of Western Civilization*. Chicago: Open Court, 2000. Kindle.

Badaracco, Joseph L., Jr. *Defining Moments: When Managers Must Choose between Right and Right*. Boston: Harvard Business Review Press, 2016. Kindle.

Barzun, Jacques. *Begin Here*. Chicago: University of Chicago Press, 1991.

Bennis, Warren, and Burt Nanus. *Leaders: The Strategies for Taking Charge*. New York: Harper and Row, 1985.

Bonhoeffer, Dietrich. *Letters and Papers from Prison*. New York: Touchstone, 1977.

Burns, James MacGregor. *Transforming Leadership*. New York: Atlantic Monthly Press, 2003.

Cameron, Julia, and Mark Bryan. *The Artists Way*. New York: G. P. Putnam's Sons, 1992.

Carlin, George. *Last Words*. New York: Simon & Schuster, 2009. Kindle.

Center for Courage & Renewal, and Shelly L. Francis. *The Courage Way: Leading and Living with Integrity*. San Francisco: Berrett-Koehler Publishers, 2018. Kindle.

Costa, John Dalia. *The Ethical Imperative*. Reading, MA: Perseus Books, 1988.

Csikszentmihalyi, Mihaly. *The Evolving Self*. New York: HarperPerennial, 1993.

Csikszentmihalyi, Mihaly. *Flow*. New York: Harper Perennial Modern Classics, HarperCollins, 2008. Kindle.

Davis, Richard A. *The Intangibles of Leadership*. Hoboken, NJ: John Wiley and Sons, 2010. Kindle.

Deresiewicz, William. *Excellent Sheep*. New York: Free Press, 2014.

Dozier, Rush, Jr. *Fear Itself*. New York: Thomas Dunne Books, 1998.

Dweck, Carol S. *Mindset*. New York: Ballantine Books, 2008.

Elmore, Tim. *Artificial Maturity*. San Francisco: Jossey-Bass Publishers, 2012.

Emerson, Ralph Waldo. *A Year with Emerson*. Edited by Richard Grossman. Boston: David R. Godine Publisher, 2003.

Erikson, Erik H. *Identity: Youth and Crisis*. New York: W. W. Norton & Company, 1968.

Frankl, Viktor E. *Man's Search for Meeting*. Beacon Press, 2006. Kindle.

Fromm, Erich. *To Have or to Be*. New York: Continuum, 2003.

Gardner, Howard. *Five Minds for the Future*. Boston: Harvard Business Press, 2009.

Gardner, Howard. *Truth, Beauty, and Goodness Reframed: Educating for the Virtues in the Age of Truth in the Age of Truthiness and Twitter*. New York: Basic Books, 2011. Kindle.

Gardner, John. *Living, Leading, and the American Dream*. San Francisco: Jossey-Bass, 2003.

Gardner, John W. *Self-Renewal: The Individual and the Innovative Society*. New York: W. W. Norton & Company, 1995.

Goens, George A. *The Fog of Reform*. Lanham, MD: Rowman & Littlefield, 2016.

Goens, George A. *It's Not My Fault: Victim Mentality and Becoming Response-able*. Lanham, MD: Rowman & Littlefield, 2017. Kindle.

Goens, George A. *Soft Leadership for Hard Times*. Lanham, MD: Rowman & Littlefield, 2005.

Goleman, Daniel. *Emotional Intelligence: Why It Can Matter More Than IQ*. New York: Random House Publishing Group, 2012. Kindle.

Gomes, Peter J. *The Good Life: Truths That Last in Times of Need*. New York: HarperCollins, 2009. Kindle.

Harris, Maxine. *The Loss That Is Forever*. New York: Penguin Books, 1995.

Havel, Vaclav. *The Art of the Impossible*. New York: Knopf Publishers, 1991.

Hedger, Chris. *Empire of Illusion*. New York: Nation Books, 2009.

Hock, Dee. *Birth of the Choardic Age*. San Francisco: Berrett-Koehler Publishers, 1999.

Jaworski, Joseph. *Synchronicity: The Inner Path of Leadership*. San Francisco: Berrett-Koehler Publishers, 1996.

Kidder, Rushworth M. *Moral Courage*. New York: HarperCollins, 2005.

Kofman, Fred. *The Meaning Revolution: The Power of Transcendent Leadership*. New York: Crown Publishing Group, 2018. Kindle.

Kubler-Ross, Elizabeth, and David Kessler. *Life Lessons*. New York: Scribner, 2000.

Leary, Mark R., ed. *Handbook for Self and Identity*. New York: Guilford Press, 2011. Kindle.

May, Rollo. *Man's Search for Himself*. New York: W. W. Norton & Company, 2009.

McCain, John. *Why Courage Matters*. New York: Random House, 2004.

Merton, Thomas. *Conjectures of a Guilty Bystander*. New York: Crown Publishing Group, 1966.

Moore, Thomas. *Care of the Soul*. New York: Harper Perennial, 1992.

O'Brien, Bill. *Character at Work*. New York: Paulist Press, 2008.

O'Donohue, John. *Eternal Echoes*. New York: HarperCollins, 1999.

O'Donohue, John. *To Bless the Space between Us*. New York: Doubleday, 2008.

O'Toole, James. *Creating the Good Life*. New York: Rodale Publishers, 2005.

Palmer, Parker J. *Let Your Life Speak*. San Francisco: Jossey-Bass Publishers, 2000.

Palmer, Parker J. *On the Brink of Everything*. Oakland, CA: Berrett-Koehler Publishers, 2018.

Paterson, Sonja, Pauline Webster, Paul Jewell, Lesley Henderson, Jill McLaughlin, and Jill Dodd. *Teaching Ethics: Care, Think and Choose: A Curriculum-based Approach to Ethical Thinking*. Cheltenham, Victoria, Australia: Hawker Brownlow Education, 2011. Kindle.

Pruett, Kyle D. *Me, Myself, and I*. New York: Goddard Press, 1991.

Robinson, Ken. *The Element*. New York: Viking Publishers, 2009.

Sanders, T. Irene. *Strategic Thinking and the New Science*. New York: Free Press, 1998.

Scharmer, C. Otto. *Theory U*. Cambridge, MA: Society for Organizational Learning. 2007.

Scharmer, C. Otto, and Katrin Kaufer. *Leading from the Emerging Future: From Ego-System to Eco-System Economies*. San Francisco: Berrett-Koehler Publishers, 2013. Kindle.

Senge, Peter M., C. Otto Scharmer, Joseph Jaworski, and Betty Sue Flowers. *Presence: An Exploration of Profound Change in People, Organizations, and Society*. New York: Crown Publishing Group, 2005. Kindle.

Sergiovanni, Thomas J. *Moral Leadership*. San Francisco: Jossey-Bass Publishers, 1992.

Singer, Irving. *Meaning in Life*. New York: Free Press, 1992.

Singer, Michael A. *The Untethered Soul: The Journey beyond Yourself*. Oakland, CA: New Harbinger Publications, 2007. Kindle.

Sternberg, Robert J. *Wisdom, Intelligence, and Creativity Synthesized*. Cambridge: Cambridge University Press, 2003.

Stoppard. Tom. *The Hard Problem*. New York: Grove Press, 2015.

Tillich, Paul. *The Courage to Be*. New Haven, CT: Yale University Press, 1952.

Vaillant, George E. *Aging Well*. Boston: Little, Brown, and Company, 2002.
Vaillant, George E. *Spiritual Evolution*. New York: Broadway Books, 2008.
Wheatley, Margaret J. *Leadership and the New Science*. San Francisco: Berrett-Koehler Publishers, 1999.
Wheatley, Margaret J. *Who Do We Choose to Be?* San Francisco: Berrett-Koehler Publishers, 2017. Kindle.
Whyte, David. *Crossing the Unknown Sea*. New York: Riverhead Books, 2001.
Whyte, David. *The Heart Aroused*. New York: Currency Doubleday, 1994.
Wilber, Ken. *Grace and Grit*. Boston: Shambhala Publications, 2000.

PERIODICALS, BLOGS, AND REPORTS

Badaracco, Joseph L., Jr. "The Discipline of Building Character." *Harvard Business Review* (March–April 1998): 4–5.
Barnett, Rosemary V. "Helping Teens Answer the Question 'Who Am I?': Cognitive Development in Adolescence." ResearchGate, 2019. https://www.researchgate.net/publication/239531192_Helping_Teens_Answer_the_Question_Who_Am_I_Cognitive_Development_in_Adolescents1.
Bower, Claire A. "From a Child's Eyes: Loss, Growth and Purpose." *Every Mother Counts* (blog), April 1, 2016. https://blog.everymothercounts.org/from-a-childs-eyes-loss-growth-and-purpose-dc986e157c72.
Buchanan, Ash. "The Purpose of Education: Becoming Yourself So You Can Contribute to Society." *The Medium*, July 10, 2016.
Christiansen, David S., and Robin Boneck. "Four Questions for Analyzing the Right-versus-Right Dilemmas of Managers." *Journal of Basic Case Studies* 6, no. 3 (May/June 2010): 54–55.
Dobrin, Arthur. "The Astonishing Power of Social Pressure." *Psychology Today*, April 14, 2014. https://www.psychologytoday.com/us/experts/arthur-dobrin-dsw.
Eckhart, Meister. Eckhart Society. https://www.eckhartsociety.org.
Evans, Sydney. "How to Define Your Defining Moments." *Forbes*, August 3, 2017. https://www.forbes.com/sites/forbescoachescouncil/2017/08/03/how-to-define-your-defining-moments/#4608aea725d0.
Frontline. "Generation Like." https://www.pbs.org/wgbh/frontline/film/generation-like/.
Glubb, Sir John. "The Fate of Empires and Search for Survival." 1976. http://people.uncw.edu/kozloffm/glubb.pdf.
Goleman, Daniel. "What Makes a Leader?" *Harvard Business Review* (November–December 1998).
Hostetler, Karl, Margaret A. Macintyre Latta, and Loukia K. Sarroub. "Retrieving Meaning in Teacher Education: The Question of Being." DigitalCommons@University of Nebraska–Lincoln, May 14, 2007. http://digitalcommons.unl.edu/teachlearnfacpub/26.
Hougaard, Rasmus, and Jacqueline Carter. "The Mindful Leader." *Rotman Management* (Fall 2018): 33–37.
"In Depth: Jacques Barzun." *Booktv*, C-Span2, May 6, 2001. https://www.youtube.com/watch?v=Nbpg0fqfL1w.
Jobs, Steve. Commencement Address. Stanford University, June 12, 2005. http://news.stanford.edu/2005/06/14/jobs-061505.
LaFlaur, Mark. "The Writing Life." *Los Angeles Times*, May 21, 2000. http://articles.latimes.com/2000/may/21/books/bk-32271.
McLeod, Saul. "Carl Rogers." Simply Psychology. https://www.simplypsychology.org/carl-rogers.html.
Morris, Pam. "Inside Every Person You Know, There Is a Person You Don't Know: The Reflection in the Mirror." https://letterpile.com/inspirational/httphubpagescomhub-The-Reflection-in-my-Mirror.

Pew Research Center. "Americans See Different Expectations for Men and Women." December 5, 2017. http://www.pewsocialtrends.org/2017/12/05/americans-see-different-expectations-for-men-and-women/.

Pew Research Center. "The Generation Gap in American Politics." March 1, 2018. http://assets.pewresearch.org/wp-content/uploads/sites/5/2018/03/01122435/03-01-18-Generations-release.pdf.

Pew Research Center. "How Millennials Today Compare with Their Grandparents 50 Years Ago." March 16, 2018. http://www.pewresearch.org/fact-tank/2018/03/16/how-millennials-compare-with-their-grandparents/.

Pew Research Center. "Teens, Social Media & Technology 2018." May 31, 2018. http://www.pewinternet.org/2018/05/31/teens-social-media-technology-2018/.

Popova, Maria. "Nietzsche on How to Find Yourself and the True Value of Education." Brain Pickings. https://www.brainpickings.org/2015/09/30/nietzsche-find-yourself schopenhauer-as-educator/.

Rumsfeld, Donald. "DoD News Briefing," February 12, 2002. http://archive.defense.gov/Transcripts/Transcript.aspx?TranscriptID=2636.

Savolainen, T., and P. Lopez-Fresno. "Trust as Intangible Asset: Enabling Intellectual Capital Development by Leadership for Vitality and Innovativeness." *Electronic Journal of Knowledge Management* 11, no. 3 (2013): 244–55. http://www.ejkm.com/issue/download.html?idArticle=407.

Schulman, Tom, screenwriter. *Dead Poets Society*. Touchstone Pictures. A Peter Weir Film, 1989.

Solly, Meilan. "US Life Expectancy Drops for Third Year in a Row, Reflecting Rising Drug Overdoses, Suicides." *Smithsonian*, December 3, 2018. https://www.smithsonianmag.com/smart-news/us-life-expectancy-drops-third-year-row-reflecting-rising-drug-overdose-suicide-rates-180970942/.

INDEX

ABOUT THE AUTHOR

George A. Goens, PhD, is a prominent author, dynamic leader, recognized educator, and featured speaker. He has written seven books and coauthored four on leadership, school reform, education, and social issues. He has also presented seminars and workshops on leadership, school reform, and leading in a crisis at regional and state conferences and for organizations and school districts across the country.
https://www.georgegoens.com/